FOR MY PARENTS
NICHOLAS AND VICTORIA,
AND, ABOVE ALL, FOR MY
WONDERFUL SISTER HOLLY,
WHO PUTS EVERYTHING
INTO PERSPECTIVE

Quadrille
PUBLISHING

Photography by
Sasha Wilkins

Additional photography
by Lisa Linder

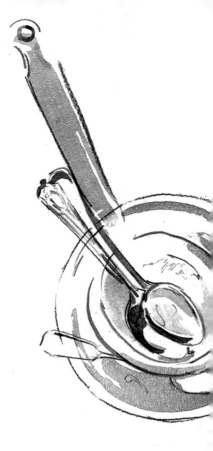

FRIENDS
FOOD
FAMILY

RECIPES AND SECRETS FROM
LIBERTYLONDONGIRL

SASHA WILKINS

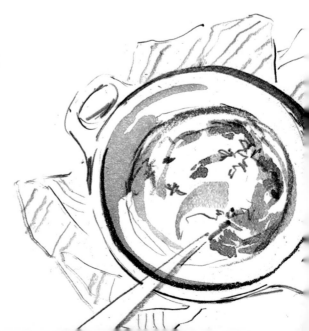

COOKERY NOTES

• Butter is salted unless otherwise stated.

• Either caster or granulated sugar can be used unless otherwise stated.

• Eggs are medium unless otherwise stated, and I always recommend using free-range, organic eggs whenever possible.

• I recommend using unwaxed citrus fruits when grating the zest.

• Recipes were tested in a fan-assisted oven. If using a regular oven, follow manufacturer's advice for adjusting temperatures.

• 1 dsp (dessertspoon) is equal to 2 tsp (teaspoons), and 1 tbsp (tablespoon) is equal to 3 tsp.

Publishing Director: Jane O'Shea
Creative Director: Helen Lewis
Senior Editor: Céline Hughes
Designer: Nicola Ellis
Illustrator: Heather Gately
Photographers: Sasha Wilkins and Lisa Linder
Prop Stylist for Special Photography: Iris Bromet
Production: Vincent Smith, Sasha Hawkes

First published in 2014 by
Quadrille Publishing Limited
Alhambra House
27–31 Charing Cross Road
London WC2H 0LS
www.quadrille.co.uk

Text © 2014 Sasha Wilkins
All photography © 2014 Sasha Wilkins except:
Pages 1, 4, 7, 19, 29, 34, 35, 37, 40, 45, 53, 61,
71, 85, 90, 93, 105, 107, 109, 115, 116, 126, 129,
141 144, 145, 157, 158, 160, 168, 174, 176, 180,
182, 192 © 2014 Lisa Linder
Design and layout © 2014 Quadrille
Publishing Limited

Cataloguing in Publication Data: a catalogue
record for this book is available from the
British Library.

ISBN: 978 184949 470 0

Printed in China

CONTENTS

SECRETS OF SUCCESSFUL ENTERTAINING

Nothing has surprised me more than the success of my blog LibertyLondonGirl. It was only ever meant to be my diary when I moved from London to New York back in 2007, so that my family and friends could stay up to date with my new life in America.

Much to my initial surprise the subject of food and entertaining has always been one of the most popular threads across all of LibertyLondonGirl, from advice posts – maybe the best place to buy cannoli in Manhattan's Little Italy – to copious recipes, always developed by me, and usually inspired by what I found in the market or in my fridge that day, via Instagrams of table settings.

When it comes to the food part, I am not a chef: I am a cook. And I have been since the age of four when my mother first taught me how to roll out pastry, with a tiny wooden rolling pin from my Galt children's baking set, a present from my godmother Rachel. Thanks to them, it seemed natural to spend as much time as I could in the kitchen when I was growing up, and so all my earliest memories (from the 1970s) revolve around food.

Those memories include watching my mother make chicken liver pâtés in deep stoneware bowls to sell in the local deli; coming home from school on Wednesday to discover every kitchen surface covered in wire racks of cooling cakes and biscuits from Delia Smith's *Book of Cakes*; the endless files of cut-out newspaper recipes to thumb through by Marika Hanbury-Tenison, Katie Stewart, Jane Grigson, Josceline Dimbleby, Caroline Conran et al.; and packed lunches that my school friends thought bizarre, including chunks of fresh mozzarella cheese, cold slices of gratins, homemade pizza, and olives.

So it's not surprising that I equate food with happiness, and that feeding my friends and family is my favourite occupation.

Wherever I find myself in the world, I cook for my friends and the people that I meet along the way. Of course, it's a challenge: getting used to new kitchens, different ingredients, cooking with whatever you can find. On my last road trip in California, I travelled with a box of kitchen essentials in the boot of my car, and I will never forget sugar pouring out of a pocket in my backpack on the luggage rack onto a passenger's head on an overnight coach journey in Australia. Some of my most memorable meals have been cooked in the most unexpected places: a youth hostel by the Golden Gate Bridge with raccoons sitting by the window, a friend's house right on Venice Beach, a children's home in Singapore, a hotel kitchen in New Delhi.

My biggest culinary shock was New York. I'd heard all the stories about Manhattan kitchens and their shoebox proportions but nothing really prepares you for a cooking space less than a metre wide – and that includes the storage. It was a real test. Not least because I'd designed and had fitted my perfect London kitchen just a year before I moved to New York. But I learnt to adapt, and honed my recipes so that they could be prepared with minimum fuss – and with the minimum of kitchen tools.

Now I am based back in London, I once again have my collection of cooking equipment around me so I can feed people on a far larger scale. Because we eat. And eat properly. I utterly refute the cry of 'nothing tastes as good as skinny feels'. Goodness, life would be so unutterably boring without delicious things to eat. I find it hard to admire

people who pick at food or remain resolutely opposed to eating.

Don't get me wrong; I watch my weight as much as the next person (there's a fine dividing line between perky and porky), but food should be a pleasure. And I hope that is what readers will take away from this book.

My hope is that the book will help the reader rustle up a meal anywhere from a beach house in Cornwall to a youth hostel kitchen somewhere idyllic, via the tiniest of Manhattan apartments, whether using food from the back of the fridge or from a fancy food hall, all the while making the people around the table feel relaxed, happy and well fed.

I'm not into napkin origami, and I don't obsess about matching plates. I am as likely to serve my cakes as fat slices wrapped in greaseproof paper, as am I am to decorate them with crystallised violets on a vintage cake stand. My soups work just as well in a vacuum flask up a mountain, as they do in porcelain bowls with matching saucers.

Above all I believe that it is the atmosphere that we create around our food that matters, not the place or the manner in which it is served (although that's not to say that I don't love a starched tablecloth when one comes my way).

I am definitely the modern type of hostess: I run my own home, I live alone and I earn my own money, but I don't think there's anything wrong with embracing domesticity, with making people feel comfortable in the environment you create around them. Whether that environment has flowers picked from your garden and plonked in a jug, or the result of spending hours at Covent Garden market and arranging perfect vases, the net result is that a happy host when entertaining makes for happy guests.

I cannot abide the kind of home entertaining that requires four different kinds of fork and plates of food that have been endlessly tweaked and smeared and garnished. Most people are just deliriously happy to be fed by someone else, and if they wanted Michelin grandeur then they would be sitting in a starred establishment in a party frock, not lolling around a friend's kitchen table, sucking up a Bloody Mary and gossiping.

So I like to serve simple food, using carefully thought out ingredients that allow me to spend as much time talking to my friends and family as I do sweating over the stove.

It always worries me when people say they don't know how to cook. It shouldn't be treated like rocket science: it's just food, the stuff we eat each and every day to keep us strong and healthy. Likewise when I see friends and readers get their kickers in a twist about entertaining: a few simple tricks and I hope you will never worry again about the colour of your napkins or candles.

I draw the line at ready meals, and processed food (beyond baked beans and ramen noodles when truly desperate) doesn't appeal to me, so even when I am running around like a headless chicken, I try to throw something together. On an average day, I set a limit of twenty minutes for prep and cooking, and it's surprising how much you can make in that time frame.

I don't pretend to have all the answers in the kitchen and in the dining room. But what I do have is a headful of recipes, and ways to serve up delicious food, that is kind to your body and to your budget.

BREAKFASTS, BRUNCHES AND BURGERS

I never really understood brunch until I moved to Manhattan, where brunch isn't just a meal — it's a way of life. There are blogs and books dedicated to charting the best places to grab your eggs and New Yorkers think nothing of lining up for as long as an hour to eat at the latest hot spot.

That being said, I do not love brunch in New York restaurants. It's not the ritual that's at fault, but the mediocre food served by restaurants that have no business to be serving eggs Benedict and Mimosas, at vastly inflated prices, to endless lines of grumpy, hungry people. Even the couscous place opposite my old St Mark's Place apartment was at it.

Never will I understand the New Yorker's fervent desire to stand in a line for 60 minutes just to eat, in a city that has a restaurant every 50 yards. Insanity.

But I do love meeting friends at the weekend for leisurely, late breakfasts that morph into lunches; the buzz and the chatter; the paper-reading and the Bloody Marys. So, my solution to avoiding the queues is to cook it myself.

Breakfast is possibly my favourite meal of the day (I always wake up with a rumbling stomach) and I've never drawn a line in the menu over what makes suitable morning food. I loved living in Singapore where breakfast is so often a bowl of chilli-spiked noodles. That's probably why the concept of brunch is so appealing: I can eat whatever I want and still think of it as breakfast.

I think my love of breakfast is partly down to my fascination with American diners, where the definition of breakfast is also elastic. Whether you want a classic burger or a short stack of pancakes, granola, or waffles and whipped cream, a diner can and will serve you.

In this chapter I've pulled together a few of my favourite breakfast and brunch ideas, and, because so many of them are inspired by the food I've eaten in American diners, there's my homage to the diner, too.

BUTTERMILK PANCAKES

We never had pancakes for breakfast, growing up, but my five years in America introduced me to the joy of a short stack with melted butter, syrup cascading down the sides, and berries and icing sugar decorating the whole. It's a fine way to start the day. If you really wanted to go the whole American hog, then strips of very crispy, streaky bacon would not go astray either.

Pancakes are perfect for serving to large mixed groups, as both children and adults love them. I have seen plenty of parents nicking bits from their kids' plates when they think no one is watching.

If you get cracking just before everyone sits down then you will thank yourself, because most people will eat at least three of these. Fortunately, they are resilient beasts, and won't suffer too badly if left for a few minutes, whilst you get on with the rest.

I like to make mine more the size of a large Scotch pancake, to which these are a close cousin, rather than the plate-sized ones I've often been served in the Mid-West.

MAKES 10–12
3 eggs
175ml buttermilk
175g plain flour
pinch of salt
1 heaped tsp baking powder
1 dsp sunflower oil

SECRET
If you don't have buttermilk, simply mix 1 tablespoon of lemon juice into 175ml of whole milk.

METHOD

It's the work of moments to prepare the batter, which you can do the night before. Beat together the eggs and the buttermilk, or milk and lemon juice. Sift together the dry ingredients in a separate bowl. Now add the liquid ingredients to the sifted dry ones and whisk together with a balloon whisk until smooth.

Add the oil to a frying pan and heat. Spoon the batter into the pan to make circle roughly 9cm in diameter. Don't be tempted to make more than 2 or 3 simultaneously, as the oil temperature will drop and the pancakes will be soggy.

Flip the pancakes when the tops are still liquid and you can see a few bubbles. These are a practice-makes-perfect thing: after making a couple you'll be able to judge when to do the flip: usually earlier than you might think. You are aiming for a nicely browned bottom.

TOPPINGS

- BLUEBERRIES AND MAPLE SYRUP
- NUTELLA AND BANANAS
- STRAWBERRIES AND WHIPPED CREAM
- APPLE SAUCE AND GROUND CINNAMON
- PECANS AND MAPLE SYRUP
- CHOCOLATE CHIPS

1 THE WOLSELEY
160 Piccadilly, W1J 9EB
www.thewolseley.com

2 CECCONI'S
5A Burlington Gardens, W1S 3EP
www.cecconis.co.uk

3 DEAN STREET TOWNHOUSE
69-71 Dean Street, W1D 3SE
www.deanstreettownhouse.com

4 BALTHAZAR
6 Russell Street, WC2B 5HZ
www.balthazarlondon.com

5 THE DELAUNAY
55 Aldwych, WC2B 4BB
www.thedelaunay.com

FIVE LONDON RESTAURANTS
for smart breakfasts

FRENCH BROCANTES

Spending several weeks each summer in rural France, in the Vienne, has given me a passion for French junk shops and the **brocantes** (vintage markets) and **vide-greniers** (literally, empty-attics) that pop up most weekends. Keep an eye out when in the car, as they are often advertised with kerbside placards. **www.vide-greniers.org** also covers *brocantes* and *marchés aux puces* (flea markets). It's an excellent resource and handy for checking out what's on when.

My favourite secret junk shop is the **Dépôt-Vente La Fauvette** in Châtellerault, France which has 900 square metres of, well, second-hand everything, including china and glass.

35 rue Jean de la Fontaine, 86100 Châtellerault, Vienne; open Thursday, Friday and Saturday 9.30am to 12pm and 2.30pm to 7pm; Sunday 2.30pm to 7pm; www.depot-vente-la-fauvette.fr

Just a block from the seafront, the alluring flower and food markets on the pretty **Cours Saleya in old Nice** make space for an antiques-and-vintage market every Monday. It's particularly good for traditional ceramics, travel ephemera and prints.

Open Monday 6am to 6pm

Les Puces de Canal, France's second biggest flea market, just outside Lyon, has a mixture of indoor permanent stands, and outdoor stalls. Given its regional setting, it's the place to pick up horticultural and outdoor collectables.

1 rue du Canal, 69100 Villeurbanne, Lyons; open Thursday and Saturday 7am to 12pm, Sunday 7am to 2pm; www.pucesducanal.com

POMEGRANATE, PLUM AND YOGURT PARFAITS

I love autumn; it's my favourite season. Wrapped up in warm clothes, but with the sun still shining, I tramp around London's parks with the sausage dog prancing in front, looking forward to eating soups and cake and pies and plums.

Which brings me to my autumnal breakfast.

I eat yogurt every day: in the summer with peaches and strawberries; in autumn with blackberries and plums and pomegranates. I add rolled oats, nuts and seeds. (Granola is great. Try my no-raisin take on page 16).

It may seem like I'm just filling space by writing a recipe for something as simple as a dish of yogurt and fruit for breakfast. But if you can spend five minutes, instead of three, layering it all up in a glass, then you have something truly delightful as opposed to just alright. And, if you are going to focus on eating healthily, it's amazing how much more appetising a dish can be if it looks good.

In this case, the presentation really does make it taste better. Here's why: layering the ingredients in advance allows the flavours to mingle. The yogurt softens the oats so they become easier to digest, and the plums start to leach their sticky, yellow juice into the yogurt. The sweet ooze of the plums contrasts perfectly with the slightly mouth-puckering, crunchy pomegranate seeds.

SERVES 4
1 pomegranate
500g plain yogurt
100g rolled oats
25g sunflower seeds
4 ripe plums, chopped
   (Victorias, in an ideal world)

METHOD

Pick 4 pretty water glasses.

The quickest way to remove seeds from a pomegranate is to halve the fruit first. Then take a wooden spoon and bang the outside of each half over a bowl; the seeds will fall out.

In each glass, place a layer of chopped plums, yogurt and oats, followed by more yogurt and plums, then top with more oats and the pomegranate seeds.

Done.

Leave for 5–10 minutes (but overnight would be wonderful) if you can, to let the flavours mingle. If you like, add a drizzle of honey. Your call.

FULL-OF-GOOD-THINGS, NO-RAISINS GRANOLA

I do not like dried fruit in my granola or muesli and I'm not a fan of ingesting hundreds of sugar-filled calories in my cereal either. I developed this version for my rather specific tastes and it turns out that I am not alone, because the first version of this recipe has been enduringly popular on my website. (Of course, if you like dried fruit in your granola, feel free to add it.)

My granola addiction dates back to very recent times. In California's Wine Country for the wedding of my dear friends Jill and Michael, I wandered into a café on Calistoga's main street looking for something breakast-y. There wasn't much on the menu, bar a bowl of granola, so I ordered it. I don't like cereal as a rule, and especially not sweet cereal, so I prepared to grit my teeth. Imagine my surprise when I thoroughly enjoyed my heaping bowl of granola – it was crunchy, unsweetened, and wholly delicious, and now that I have worked out how to make my own, I eat it in shovelfuls.

Traditionally, apple juice is used to moisten the mix, but my secret ingredient is elderflower cordial, which gives an elusive floral note. I also use a packet of multigrain porridge mix containing oats, barley, spelt and toasted rye flakes, to avoid multiple half-full packages of grains in the larder.

MAKES 1KG
1 dsp runny honey
2 dsp agave nectar
1 dsp maple syrup
120ml warm water
60ml elderflower cordial
60ml apple juice
1kg mixed grains and seeds
  (I generally use a 750g box of grain mix, and make up the other 250g with: 2 dsp chia seeds, 3 dsp ground flaxseeds, approx. 65g sunflower seeds, approx. 70g nibbed hazelnuts)

METHOD
Preheat the oven to 120°C/250°F/gas mark ½.

In a small saucepan, heat up the honey, agave nectar, maple syrup and water. Then add the elderflower cordial and apple juice.

When it's all warm and flowing nicely, pour over your grain mixture, forming it into clumps with your hands. (Clumps are good as they give you extra crunch.) If you eat a bit now and it tastes quite sweet, do not worry – that sweetness disappears upon cooking. It should smell like a warm hamster cage.

Scoop the mixture out onto 2 or 3 large, flat baking trays, squishing it in your hands and making sure it has lots of little clumps and balls. It's important not to have a layer that's too thick, or it won't crisp properly. Bake in the oven for about 45 minutes. Every 15 minutes or so, take the trays out and shake the granola about so that it cooks evenly.

I prefer mine quite brown so it's really crunchy – I recommend tasting as you go to see what you prefer.

That's it. Leave it on the tray to cool, then scoop into sterilised, airtight jars. (See page 114 for more information on sterilising jars.)

SWEETCORN, CHEESE AND BACON MUFFINS

Savoury muffins aren't nearly as common on this side of the Atlantic as they are in America: when I lived in California, friends would make batches and freeze them, using them as a convenient, on-the-hoof breakfast.

That being said, it's also very satisfying pulling apart a muffin, warm from the oven, and slathering over butter, which then melts down your chin.

MAKES 8

3 tsp baking powder
250g plain flour
3 tbsp single cream
3 eggs
120g tinned sweetcorn
100g Cheddar, grated
100g bacon, snipped into small pieces
sea salt and freshly ground black pepper
muffin tin, lined with 8 paper muffin cases

METHOD

Preheat the oven to 180°C/350°F/gas mark 4.

Mix together the baking powder and flour.

In a separate bowl, beat together the cream and eggs with the sweetcorn, cheese and bacon, along with a generous pinch of salt and a grind of black pepper.

In a large mixing bowl, combine all the ingredients.

This is a sticky dough, so it is helpful to use a large ice-cream scoop to measure accurate amounts for each muffin. Divide the mixture between the paper cases and bake for 20 minutes.

Tip the muffins out of the tin and allow to cool on a wire rack.

SECRET

Try switching around the fillings: I love spinach and feta, and sun-blush tomatoes and fresh herbs are good, too.

FRENCH TOAST (OR EGGY BREAD)

French toast has always been a morning classic in my household, whether savoury or sweet. Also known as eggy bread (which horrifies my American friend, Steve, who thinks it smacks too much of the nursery so, of course, I delight in only calling it eggy bread in his presence) it is simply fresh or stale bread soaked in seasoned, beaten egg and fried – although I have a suggestion here for baking it, which I prefer.

Count on one egg per slice of bread. Most people will eat two slices (I find guests can be bottomless pits where French toast is concerned).

Break the eggs into a bowl and beat with a fork. For savoury French toast, add a pinch of salt; for sweet, add a heaped teaspoon of white caster sugar.

Slice the bread thickly, and cut off the crusts. Dip the bread thoroughly in the egg, a piece at a time, making sure it is saturated and soggy with beaten egg. Soak for longer if it is stale or if you like very thick slices.

Add a couple of tablespoons of cooking oil to a large frying pan and heat it until it smokes. Turn the extractor fan onto high. (This dish is going to spread frying smells everywhere otherwise.) Slide two pieces at a time into the frying pan (too much cools down the oil and the toast will be soggy).

I like French toast quite browned and very crispy, but if you want a lighter colour, keep checking the bottom of the bread and then flip it over when done to your liking, to cook the reverse side.

Flip it out of the frying pan and onto kitchen paper to drain off some of the oil. Arrange beautifully on a plate.

And – the pièce de résistance – I then add a fine layer of Marmite to my French toast. I do realise that some of you now think I am the wrong-est person in the world for doing this. All I can say is: don't knock it until you've tried it. Otherwise, try it as an accompaniment to an English breakfast or, if you've gone down the sweet route, try fresh fruit, icing sugar and whipped cream.

BAKED FRENCH TOAST
I made this by accident one day when I was staring into the frying pan, thinking that it was a shame you needed so much oil to make French toast successfully. Wondering what would happen if I baked it, I popped a roasting tin with 2 tablespoons vegetable oil in the oven at 180°C/350°F/gas mark 4, to heat.

When the oil was heated, I slipped in four slices of egg-soaked bread and shut the oven door. Imagine my surprise when I checked in ten minutes later to discover my bread all puffed up like a Yorkshire pudding. Success! I checked the bottoms of the slices and discovered delectably crispy bottoms.

Baked French toast is most successful with bread that is extra-thick-sliced – at least 2cm. The longer the soaking time the better – twenty minutes is perfect.

CORNISH FRENCH TOAST
This is so many ways of righteous wrong. It was an idea born when I was staying in a holiday rental in Cornwall. Our hosts had left us free-range eggs, bread, jam and clotted cream. So, when it came to cooking breakfast next morning, I suppose I could have made poached eggs. But I was on holiday, the sun was shining and that clotted cream was singing a siren song from the fridge. Make your French toast as normal, and then pile on the jam and cream.

INDIAN FRENCH TOAST
This stratospherically wonderful version requires the egg to be beaten with about 25ml milk, a pinch of salt, a finely chopped green chilli and half a chopped onion, then soaking the bread in the mixture before frying.

BAKED EGGS
WITH MUSHROOMS

My Warwickshire grandmother, Granny Horse, had a set of Royal Worcester china egg coddlers when I was a little girl. They fascinated me to the point where she gave in and cooked me a coddled egg. I can't say I was that impressed: essentially, what she served me was an extremely runny poached egg.

Once I could cook for myself I did my own experimenting: a coddled egg is an egg cooked in a closed-top, buttered, china vessel, so it poaches very, very gently and the egg white never goes rubbery. I played around and discovered that I much preferred the French approach – poaching them in a ramekin that is surrounded by water, 'en cocotte'.

I'm not going to pretend these are a healthy breakfast option. Instead, I'm going to revel in their sheer, indulgent deliciousness: they are very, very rich.

If you aren't keen on mushrooms, simply leave them out. (You could substitute chopped ham.)

SERVES 4
250g mushrooms
3 spring onions
approx. 20g butter
½ garlic clove, chopped
handful soft green herbs, chopped (I like chervil, chives, thyme and oregano), plus extra, to serve
sea salt and freshly ground black pepper
4 eggs
4 dsp double cream
50g Parmesan, grated
4 slices of toast, to serve
4 ovenproof ramekins

METHOD
Preheat the oven to 180°C/350°F/gas mark 4.

Very finely chop the mushrooms and the spring onions (use half the green parts), and fry them until soft in a generous amount of butter over a medium heat with the garlic and the fresh herbs.

Divide the mixture between 4 ramekins, add salt and pepper and carefully break an egg over the mushrooms.

Pour over the double cream and sprinkle over the grated cheese.

Place the ramekins in a roasting tin and pour boiling water around them to 1cm under the lip. Cook for about 10 minutes.

Sprinkle over some black pepper and a few chopped herbs and eat with toast.

FAVOURITE AMERICAN DINERS

SOMETIMES YOU JUST WANT TO SIT
AT A COUNTER AND ORDER COFFEE
AND A BURGER. MAYBE EGGS.
AND POSSIBLY A DANISH ...

B&H DAIRY
127 2nd Avenue, New York

A KOSHER DINER. AND MY OLD MANHATTAN
BREAKFAST HAUNT. STILL OPERATIONAL. AFTER
SIXTY-FIVE YEARS IN BUSINESS, IT'S BECOME AN
EAST VILLAGE INSTITUTION. CHEAP AS CHIPS.
THEIR CHALLAH FRENCH TOAST IS WORTH
TRAVELLING FOR.

THE 11TH STREET DINER
South Beach, Miami

OPEN 24 HOURS A DAY AND HOUSED IN AN
ORIGINAL ART-DECO DINING CAR. MAKE SURE
YOU ORDER A SIDE OF FLORIDA AVOCADO WITH
EVERYTHING YOU EAT.
WWW.ELEVENTHSTREETDINER.COM

SWINGERS DINER
*820 Beverly Boulevard,
Los Angeles*

SIT AT THE COUNTER AT THIS TRAD DINER IN THE
HEART OF BEVERLY HILLS AND ENJOY SOME
GRADE-A PEOPLE-WATCHING: ACTORS, LOVERS,
GRANNIES, DATES ... WWW.SWINGERSDINER.COM

IT'S TOPS COFFEE SHOP
*1801 Market Street,
San Francisco*

I'M NOT SURE WHETHER I LOVE THE NAME OR THE
PEPTO-BISMOL-PINK WAITRESS UNIFORMS MORE ...
WWW.ITSTOPSCOFFEESHOP.COM

EGGS WITH CHICKPEA PUREE AND FLATBREAD

I ate something similar to this for breakfast in Marrakesh and fell hard for the earthiness of chickpeas against creamy, runny eggs, whether scrambled, fried or poached. Chilli sauce would be more than acceptable here, too. For a delicious, quick, satisfying breakfast, this is hard to beat.

SERVES 2

400g tin chickpeas, drained (reserve some liquid)
2 tbsp olive oil
1 garlic clove, peeled
good handful coriander or flat-leaf parsley leaves
sea salt and freshly ground black pepper
4 eggs
2 large flatbreads

METHOD

In a food processor, whizz up the chickpeas with a little of the liquid from their tin, 1 tbsp of the olive oil, the garlic, coriander leaves and some salt and pepper.

Now choose how to cook your eggs, whether fried (as pictured above), poached (see page 26), or as follows: in a frying pan, heat the rest of the olive oil, break in the eggs and gently stir with a fork until lightly cooked. (They aren't supposed to be scrambled, more like a cross between fried eggs and an omelette.)

To serve, put a dollop of the chickpea purée on the plate, slide on the eggs and garnish the lot with some of the chopped herbs. Serve with the flatbreads.

FIVE LONDON RESTAURANTS AND CAFES FOR BRUNCH

THE BREAKFAST CLUB
(Soho, Angel, Hoxton, Spitalfields, Battersea Rise and London Bridge)
www.thebreakfastclubcafes.com

THE RIDING HOUSE CAFE
43–51 Great Titchfield Street, W1W 7PQ
www.ridinghousecafe.co.uk

KOPAPA
32–34 Monmouth Street, WC2H 9HA
www.kopapa.co.uk

THE MODERN PANTRY
47–48 St John's Square, EC1V 4JJ
www.themodernpantry.co.uk

LANTANA
13 Charlotte Place, W1T 1SN
www.lantanacafe.co.uk

SATURDAY-MORNING OMELETTE TORTILLA WRAP

I eat these the morning after the night before: they are filling, very savoury for a deadened palate, quite low in carbs and packed full of vegetables and protein in a not-too-worthy manner.

They are simply two-egg omelettes, topped with mushrooms, spring onions and cheese, rolled up in a tortilla and eaten with fingers – and gusto.

METHOD

Heat 1 tbsp of the olive oil in a small frying pan and gently cook the mushrooms and the spring onions until soft. Season with salt and black pepper.

Reserve on a plate. Put a little more oil in the empty mushroom pan.

Beat the eggs and season with salt and black pepper before pouring into the pan. Let the bottom set, and then use a fork to lift the edges and swirl the uncooked egg underneath to set. (This is a very thin omelette.)

When the top looks cooked, add the mushrooms and spring onions. Scatter the cheese and chopped chives over the top.

Heat up a second frying pan, place a tortilla in it and slide in the cooked omelette over the tortilla.

After a minute or so, when the tortilla is both warm and softened by the heat, slide it onto a plate and roll up. Then take a very sharp, non-serrated knife and cut into 3 pieces.

I like to eat these with ample amounts of Sriracha chilli sauce.

SERVES 1

1–2 tbsp olive oil
5 mushrooms, sliced
2 spring onions, sliced
diagonally
sea salt and freshly ground
black pepper
2 eggs
50g hard cheese, grated,
or soft cheese (any cheese
will do really)
1 tbsp chopped chives
1 medium tortilla or wrap

HUEVOS RANCHEROS

Whilst I am a strong advocate of a big platter of food in the centre of the table that my guests can dive into, helping themselves to the bits that they favour, there are some dishes that just work better one-on-one, so to speak.

Huevos rancheros, with its piled-high layering of tortilla, salsa, beans, avocado and fried eggs is the perfect individual plate: colourful, appealing and delicious. That being said, I've eaten some unappealing versions, some reduced to just eggs, salsa and tortilla; others ruined by pallid yolks, watery tomatoes or tasteless beans. Like any simple dish – it takes a scant 30 minutes to prep and cook – huevos rancheros only works when the ingredients are good in the first place.

I'm not going to pretend this is an echt huevos rancheros. But it tastes damn good, looks delicious (sometimes this dish can look like roadkill) and has all the key ingredients. I've purposely kept the chilli count low because so many people don't like the burn, but that's nothing a good dash of hot sauce can't put right.

SERVES 4

6 medium tomatoes
1 small onion
bunch coriander leaves,
  chopped
1 lime
sea salt and freshly ground
  black pepper
oil, for frying
2 tsp ground cumin
1 garlic clove, crushed
400g tin pinto or black beans,
  drained, or refried beans
Tabasco or hot sauce
4 tortillas
4–8 large eggs
200g cheese (I use Monterey
  Jack if I can find it, otherwise
  Cheddar will do), grated
125g sour cream
Four-Minute Guacamole
  (see page 170)

METHOD

Roughly chop the tomatoes, removing their cores, and finely chop the onion. Add to a bowl with about 1 tbsp of the chopped coriander, a squeeze of lime and a little salt and mix together.

Heat 1 dsp olive oil, add the cumin and fry for a few seconds, before adding the crushed garlic, beans, enough water to fill half the empty can and a dash of Tabasco or hot sauce. Mix together thoroughly, mashing the beans, and simmer away gently until everything else is ready.

Heat each tortilla in a dry frying pan for 1 minute or so each side until they start to puff and brown. Reserve in a warm oven or at the back of the stove.

Finally, fry 1–2 eggs per person, depending on greed.

To serve, put a warm tortilla on each plate. Spoon over the beans and the tomato salsa, side by side.

Sprinkle over the grated cheese and slide on the fried eggs.

Put a very large dollop of sour cream on one side and the same of guacamole on the other. Liberally sprinkle with chopped coriander. Eat.

SECRET
This goes very well with Bloody Marys.

ESSENTIAL
KITCHEN EQUIPMENT

Whilst most cooks could produce delicious things from their kitchen with just a frying pan, saucepan, chopping board, a single sharp knife and a wooden spoon, there are some bits of kit that do make life a lot easier. Things like rolling pins can always be subbed: milk bottles work well, but try cooling a cake without a wire rack ...

THESE ARE THE POSSESSIONS
I USE THE MOST:

- A digital timer and thermometer combined
- A 18cm/7inch non-stick cake tin
- Tongs
- A mandoline for slicing things very thinly
- A stand mixer – for cake batters and icing

- A food processor for grating, chopping and puréeing
- A wire rack for cooling cakes and biscuits
- A wide and high straight-sided frying pan – a sauteuse
- Silicone spatulas
- A good vegetable peeler and an apple corer
- Two sets of measuring spoons: metric and US cups
- A tiny whisk for dressings, and a large one for sauces
- A measuring jug with imperial and metric markings
- Digital scales
- A set of stainless steel mixing bowls
- A large sieve – which can double as a colander

I don't use them as often, but a salad spinner, a silicone pastry brush and a pestle and mortar are great investments.

THE EASIEST POACHED EGGS, WITH SPINACH PURÉE AND MUFFINS

For anyone reading this who has the fear where poached eggs are concerned, read on: I have found the solution.

For years, poached eggs have been my downfall in the kitchen. I have tried whirlpools, which never whirled enough; vinegar, which made my eggs taste funny; silicone moulds, which made my eggs look like discs; and metal poachers which stuck to the eggs ... nothing, nothing worked, neatly proving my point that, however confident you are in the kitchen, there will always be something that is your cook's Achilles heel.

Then I was accidentally served a cold poached egg with my breakfast in a London restaurant and I couldn't for the life of me work out how that had happened. I looked a little closer, realised that my egg resembled a money bag, and it all became clear: they had broken the egg into a ramekin lined with clingfilm and then scrunched up the top. That meant they could poach eggs in their clingfilm shells in advance, leave them to cool and simply heat them up on demand, removing the clingfilm when done.

This has changed my poaching life: I merrily make poached eggs almost every day now. No more fear of broken yolks or ectoplasmic whites. I am such a confident egg-poacher that I happily make Eggs Florentine for brunch for friends. Well, sort of. I draw the line at making hollandaise at weekends, so I have developed my own version, which has the happy result of being less calorific and super quick.

All you have to do then is toast your muffins and poach your eggs – which you could have prepared earlier but, really, how hard is it to poach eggs to order now that you have my special, failsafe method?

SECRET
Frozen spinach is the secret here. Defrosted, it makes a great sauce when mixed with a little vegetable stock and cream or crème fraîche.

SERVES 4

250g frozen leaf spinach
 (not chopped)
60ml vegetable stock
60ml single cream
sea salt and freshly ground
 black pepper
4–8 eggs (depending on hunger
 and greed)
oil, for greasing (optional)
4 English muffins
a little butter
snipped chives, to serve
 (optional)

METHOD

Place the spinach in a saucepan, pour over the
vegetable stock and simmer until the spinach
has defrosted. Beat in the single cream and
season with salt and black pepper to taste.

Put a pan of water on to boil.

Line a ramekin with a very large square
of clingfilm, overlapping the edges. (If you
are nervous, a drop of oil in the bottom will
help ease off the clingfilm when the eggs
are cooked.)

Break an egg into the ramekin and pull up the
edges of the clingfilm to form a money bag.
Twist the top to seal. Repeat with each egg.

Lower the money bags carefully into the water,
and cook for 3 minutes for runny middles, or
5 minutes for 'œufs mollets', where the yolk is
semi-cooked.

Halve and toast the muffins and butter as
liberally as you dare.

Cut the top of each egg moneybag with a pair
of scissors and carefully peel off its clingfilm
jacket. Discard.

Dollop some spinach mixture on each plate,
add 2 muffin halves and place an egg on top.
A sprinkle of chives is good.

THE PERFECT BURGER

There are as many methods for a perfect hamburger as there are chefs on this planet. After sampling many, many burgers in my kitchen, I came to the conclusion that less is more every time. So, there are no crumbled crackers, no breadcrumbs, no Worcestershire sauce or chilli seasonings in the LLG burger. It's simply pure minced beef with a finely chopped shallot, flavoured with parsley for some pep.

You can make them as normal burgers or go down the American route and make sliders, those little two-mouthful patties that are so popular as appetisers.

We like to go traditional with our toppings, so I just add a slice of tomato, some red onion rings, a little crunchy lettuce – about the only time we find iceberg acceptable – and, sometimes, some burger sauce made from ketchup and mayo mixed together. Maybe the odd gherkin if we are in the mood.

MAKES 4 LARGE OR 6 MEDIUM BURGERS
1 shallot, finely chopped
a little butter
750g minced beef
handful flat-leaf parsley leaves,
  chopped
sea salt and freshly ground black pepper
4–6 burger buns
Burger Sauce (see page 31), optional
4–6 thick slices of tomato
4–6 leaves of crunchy lettuce, e.g. iceberg
1 red onion, cut into rings

METHOD
Gently cook the shallot in a little butter until translucent.

Mix together the shallot, mince, parsley and plenty of salt and black pepper and shape into patties with your hands. Pop in the fridge for 30 minutes.

Heat up a non-stick frying pan or griddle and slap your burger in. Cook for about 3 minutes on each side if you like them pink within, 4 for well done.

Slice the burger buns in half, spread over the Burger Sauce, if using, and sandwich with a patty, a slice of tomato, a lettuce leaf and some onion rings.

1. MUSHROOM AND HALLOUMI BURGER

Whilst I like a good bean burger, not a lot can beat the simple combination of a grilled flat mushroom, a thick slab of halloumi, a slice of tomato and some crisp lettuce leaves for the required chew. This is perfect for a weekend lunch, or for a kitchen supper with friends.

SERVES 1

1 large flat mushroom
olive oil, for frying
sea salt and freshly ground black pepper
1 thick slice of halloumi

For the burger sauce
1 tsp mayonnaise
1 tsp tomato ketchup
1 tsp Dijon mustard

METHOD

Fry the mushroom in a generous splash of olive oil over a slow heat in a small frying pan, with a lid over the top, for about 5–10 minutes. Season with salt and black pepper.

If cooking several mushrooms for several burgers, it is worth preheating the oven to 180°C/350°F/gas mark 4, popping the mushrooms in an ovenproof dish, drizzling olive oil over them, top and bottom, and stretching foil tightly over the dish. Roast them for 15–20 minutes.

Put a frying or griddle pan over a medium heat and when hot, add the halloumi. Cook for 2 minutes each side, or until lighly browned and pliable.

Mix together the burger sauce ingredients. Sandwich the halloumi and mushroom in a roll spread with the burger sauce. The best accompaniments are pesto, tomato and lettuce.

Eat. With plenty of napkins.

2. SWEETCORN FRITTER BURGER

I have yet to meet anyone, including fussy children, who does not like these. Best of all, they are extremely easy and quick to make. I particularly like them sandwiched in a roll, but they are just as good for breakfast with a poached egg, or for lunch with raita and a salad.

SERVES 4

325g tin sweetcorn (drained weight 100g)
100g plain flour
50g gram (chickpea) flour
1 tsp baking powder
large pinch of sea salt
1 grind black pepper
2 generous pinches of paprika (optional)
2 eggs
150ml milk
small handful flat-leaf parsley or coriander
** leaves, very finely chopped (optional)**
1 tbsp vegetable oil, per 2 fritters

METHOD

Drain the sweetcorn and allow to dry. Sift the flours and baking powder into a large bowl. Add the salt, pepper and paprika, if using. Beat the eggs together with the milk, and add slowly to the flour, constantly beating to form a smooth batter. Add the sweetcorn and the parsley or coriander.

Set a large frying pan over a medium-high heat, adding 1 tbsp vegetable oil. Once hot, add 2 tbsp mixture to the pan for each fritter. (Cook 2 at a time.) Smooth the mixture out and, after about 2 minutes, when the edges are bubbling, flip over to cook the other side. (The top should still be wet when flipped.) Press down on the cooked top side with a spatula to ensure the inside of the fritter cooks, otherwise, you will end up with a crispy outside and raw middle. Check the underside and, if necessary, flip again until crisp on each side.

Remove from the pan to a plate lined with kitchen paper. This is best served with caramelised onions, yogurt and lettuce in a soft roll (I like 2 per roll).

3. GLAMORGAN BURGER

The only connection that Glamorgan sausages have to their piggy counterparts is their shape: instead of being stuffed with pork, the main ingredients in these traditional Welsh sausages are Caerphilly cheese, leeks and breadcrumbs.

It's a delicious combination, which also makes a fine vegetarian burger, slapped between bread and laced with tomato ketchup. I've added some dried red chilli flakes to mine, but that's entirely optional.

SERVES 5–6

2 medium leeks
1 tsp butter
200g fresh breadcrumbs, plus an extra 100g, for the crispy coating
100g Caerphilly cheese, grated (a hard cheese like Cheddar, Lancashire or Cheshire can be subbed)
sea salt and freshly ground black pepper
½ tsp mustard powder
1 tsp dried chilli flakes (optional)
1 tbsp chopped flat-leaf parsley
3 eggs
65ml milk
approx. 4 tbsp oil, for frying

METHOD

Cut the dark green parts off the leeks, discard, and shred the whites finely by quartering lengthwise, and then cutting each quarter lengthwise again into fine strips. Cut these strips into 5cm sections.

Heat the butter in a frying pan and, when melted, add the leeks. Cook gently over a medium heat until the leeks are soft. They must not brown and will take about 10 minutes. When cooked, remove to a plate so that they can cool quickly.

Place all the dry ingredients in a large mixing bowl (breadcrumbs, grated cheese, salt, pepper, mustard powder, and chilli flakes, if using) and mix together with your hands to ensure everything is distributed evenly. Then add the cooled, cooked leeks and chopped parsley and mix again.

Beat together 2 of the eggs in a separate bowl, and then add to the dry ingredients. Mix together and then form into 5–6 hamburger-shaped patties.

Beat the last egg in a bowl with the milk. Pour the rest of the breadcrumbs into a lipped baking tray. Take a patty and place it gently in the egg mixture, then lift it out using a spatula, allowing any excess egg to drip off. Then place the patty in the breadcrumbs and flip over so it is completely covered. Make sure that the sides are breadcrumbed, too. Repeat until all the patties are coated.

Heat 2 tbsp oil in a heavy frying pan and cook the patties, 2 at a time, over a medium heat, pressing down gently to ensure the patty makes contact evenly with the base of the pan. Do not fry over too high a heat, but do make sure that they heat all the way through. They draw up quite a lot of oil so, if you prefer, bake these in a moderate oven instead. They will take about 25 minutes to warm through, and a quick flash under the grill will ensure a crisp finish.

I like to use a crispy white roll to contrast with the burger's soft middle. Cut it in half and layer up with cream cheese, spinach and chutney.

4. CAULIFLOWER AND QUINOA BURGER (GLUTEN-FREE)

Cauliflower cakes are a perfect standby for those days when you want to roll out of bed towards the stove: you can make them the night before and, as a bonus, they are less likely to fall apart in the frying pan after a few hours in the fridge. They make an excellent morning-after-the-night-before brunch, packed as they are with vitamins and good things. Note that you will need a food processor to make cauliflower rubble in this recipe. Don't forget to use gluten-free bread rolls if serving to coeliacs.

If you can find red quinoa, then a combination of half-red and half-white quinoa looks great.

MAKES 6–8

175g quinoa
250g cauliflower florets
white and green parts of 4
  spring onions, chopped
handful flat-leaf parsley or
  coriander, finely chopped
50g Parmesan, grated
grated zest of 1 lemon
sea salt and freshly ground
  black pepper
100g gram (chickpea) flour,
  plus extra for dusting
4 eggs, beaten together
plenty of sunflower or rapeseed
  oil, for frying

METHOD

Cook the quinoa according to the packet instructions, drain and leave to cool. Roughly chop the cauliflower and reduce to fine rubble in a food processor, using the pulse button.

Tip the cauliflower rubble into a large mixing bowl and add the chopped spring onions, herbs, Parmesan and lemon zest. Generously season with salt and black pepper. Sift in the gram flour and mix it all together with your hands.

Add the cooled quinoa to the mixture and mix again. Pour over the beaten eggs and really thoroughly combine. You will end up with a very, very wet mixture, but do not be disheartened. The egg is necessary to bind the mixture: as it cooks, the proteins solidify and stop the cake falling apart.

Pour a generous amount of flour onto a dinner or shallow soup plate. Take a handful of the wet mixture, form into a patty in your hands and place in the flour. Very gently lift and turn it over, so that both sides are thickly covered in flour.

Place a large frying pan over a medium-high heat, and add 1 tbsp oil. When it is smoking, slide your first 2 patties into the oil. Do not be tempted to cook more than 2 at a time, as they will lower the temperature of the oil. Press down gently with the back of a fish slice.

Flip over very carefully after about 2–3 minutes to cook the other sides. You may need to flip again to ensure an even browning. When cooked, remove to a plate lined with kitchen paper. Each pair takes about 4 minutes to cook.

These are wonderful with a poached egg on top, with a fresh tomato chutney; but best of all I like them sandwiched in a bread roll with some red onion, guacamole and cherry tomatoes.

FOOD TO EAT WHEN YOU COME IN FROM THE COLD

Sometimes I think that a large part of the pleasure in a long, winter walk is coming in from the cold, knowing that you have earned a delicious, rib-sticking treat of a meal. After all, anticipation always adds spice to the eating and the exercise earns you a big plate of something carbohydrate filled.

I think there is a particular kind of food that is perfect for eating when you are cold to the marrow; food that acts as central-heating for the body, as well as for the soul. It's going to be hot, comforting and possibly nostalgic, too.

What it won't be is complicated, cold, or time-consuming to prepare. Quite a few of these recipes can be made in advance and simply reheated when ravenous people return from the great outdoors.

A word from the wise: never undercater and remember the phrase, 'hungry as a hunter'.

SASHA'S HANGOVER CURE: FRIED GNOCCHI WITH MOZZARELLA AND CHERRY TOMATOES

This is the most popular recipe that I have ever written, a fact that still slightly bemuses me. It is particularly indulgent and very moreish. So maybe it's just the combination of salty, buttery, crispy, carb-y goodness, with the umami hit of the tomatoes that does it?

SERVES 2 GREEDY PEOPLE

1 packet vacuum-packed gnocchi
1 tbsp olive oil
25g butter
a few handfuls cherry tomatoes, halved
1 ball mozzarella cheese
handful basil leaves
sea salt and freshly ground black pepper

METHOD

Simply boil a large pan of salted water, tip in the gnocchi and cook according to the packet instructions (a few minutes).

Fish out when cooked and drain. Meanwhile, heat the olive oil and butter in a large, non-stick frying pan.

When the oil is hot, tip in the gnocchi (be careful, the oil will spit) and the tomatoes.

After about 5 minutes, when the gnocchi have started to catch and brown, add in ripped-up pieces of the mozzarella.

The temptation is to keep stirring, but you want the gnocchi to stick so that their bottoms go all crispy, so resist the temptation to keep prodding them. And if you mix it up too much, the cheese will melt into a lump of goo. (If that does happen, just use some kitchen scissors to cut it up.)

Tear the basil leaves over everything and season with salt and black pepper. Then eat. Lots.

WINTER WARMING DRINKS

A CLASSIC HOT TODDY
Into a heatproof glass, place a spoonful of honey, a squeeze of lemon and a shot of whisky. Top up with boiling water and stir (with a cinnamon stick, if you feel so moved).

INFUSED HOT APPLE JUICE
Place the zest from one orange, a teaspoon of brown sugar and three or four cloves in a saucepan and heat with 750ml apple juice (cloudy is nicest).

INDULGENT HOT CHOCOLATE WITH MARSHMALLOWS
Heat 1 litre of whole milk to a simmer, divide 150g dark chocolate drops (60–70 per cent cocoa solids) between four mugs and pour over the hot milk. Stir until melted and top with marshmallows.

CAULIFLOWER-CHEESE SOUP

Rich, creamy, intensely savoury, velvet-textured: this soup is, frankly, a hug in a mug. It's also a great way to get some vegetables into children. (My godchildren love it.)

SERVES 4–6

1 tbsp vegetable oil (groundnut or sunflower are good)
1 medium onion, chopped
1 large cauliflower (approx. 1kg)
1–1.5 litres vegetable or chicken stock
1 dsp Dijon mustard
7.1q. 200g Cheddar, grated – 2 cups
sea salt and freshly ground black pepper
1 tbsp chopped flat-leaf parsley
blender

METHOD

Find a big saucepan, pour in the oil, turn the heat to medium and throw in the onion.

Turn the heat to low-medium – the onion should cook slowly, without browning. Push the bits of onion around in a desultory way with a spatula from time to time, to check that they aren't sticking. This will take about 15 minutes.

In between prodding the onion, chop up the cauliflower into small pieces (removing the stalk and outer leaves) and, when the onion is translucently soft, throw the cauliflower rubble into the pan.

Then you need about 1 litre of stock. (It's going to depend on the volume of your pan compared with the cauliflower – the liquid should just cover the pieces.) Heat the stock in a separate pan and then pour it over the cauliflower.

Cook the cauliflower until it is soft. This will take about 10 minutes.

Use either a stick blender or goblet blender to whizz the cauliflower to a soup consistency. If using a goblet blender, return the soup to the pan. Add the mustard and the grated Cheddar and stir until it is all melted.

Check the consistency of the soup. If it looks too thin, bubble it up on the stove to reduce the liquid; equally, if too thick, add a little more stock/hot water.

Season generously to taste with lots of black pepper and salt. I sometimes add a little chopped flat-leaf parsley, or a splash of truffle oil.

CHICKEN, ORZO AND PARSLEY SOUP

Chicken goes particularly well with orzo, the tiny rice-shaped pasta, as neither overwhelms the other. That being said, this soup is full of flavour, enhanced by a splash of chilli sauce and a squeeze of lemon at the end. I like it because you can prepare the main part hours in advance, leaving only the final hotting up to do when you crash through the door, desperate for something warm to eat. That's because the labour can be divided by poaching the chicken well in advance, stripping the meat off the bone and then leaving both the stock and the meat in the fridge until 10 minutes before you want to eat it, which is all the time you need to cook the pasta in the stock.

SERVES 4

500g chicken joints
100g orzo
large handful flat-leaf parsley leaves, chopped
1½ lemons
chilli sauce (optional); I use either Sriracha, or chilli oil

METHOD

Rinse the chicken pieces under the cold tap and place in a saucepan. Cover the pieces with cold water, bring to the boil, cover and reduce the heat so that the water simmers. Cook for 45 minutes. (The chicken will be cooked after about 25, if you are in a hurry, but I like a richer stock, which comes from the longer cooking time.)

Using tongs or a slotted spoon, transfer the chicken to a chopping board to cool. Using fingers, discard the skin and remove the chicken from the bone. If it is breast, shred the meat into strips; if legs or thighs, tear into small pieces, discarding pieces of cartilage and any fatty bits.

Pour the cooking liquid through a sieve into a measuring jug, being careful to leave the cooking scum behind on the bottom of the pan. Make up the stock with hot water to 750ml, pour into a clean saucepan and bring to the boil. Add the orzo and cook until al dente. This will take around 5–6 minutes.

Add the chicken, three-quarters of the chopped parsley and a squeeze from the half lemon. Stir through the soup. Ladle out into bowls and sprinkle the remaining parsley leaves on the top. Quarter the remaining lemon. Serve with chilli sauce and the lemon quarters to hand.

WINTER-WARMING BEEF, BARLEY, MUSHROOM AND CARROT STEW

One-pot meals like stews really are a wonderful thing to come home to after a long walk in the countryside or poking around in the garden.

If you add lots of vegetables and barley then you will also have a very robust, nutritious and comforting meal. One of the best things about a stew like this is that once you master the basics, then you can ring the changes with different meats, vegetables and herbs. If you don't want to use wine, you can replace this with more stock (either make this from scratch or use bouillon powder).

SERVES 4–6

3 large carrots
2 celery sticks
1 large leek
1 large onion
1 garlic clove
250g chestnut mushrooms
3 tbsp olive oil, plus 1 dsp
750g stewing steak, cut into chunks
100g barley
200ml red wine
500ml stock of your choice
a couple of sprigs of thyme
2 bay leaves
sea salt and freshly ground black pepper

SECRET
This is one of those spectacularly good one-pot recipes that will stand you in good stead time and time again. And the leftovers will happily reheat so it's worth making a hefty batch to see you through those can't-cook/won't-cook evenings.

METHOD

Peel and chop the carrots and celery into small pieces. Slice the leek into 1cm rounds and then halve them. Chop the onion and the garlic together. Cut the mushrooms into sixths and reserve separately from the other vegetables.

Place a flameproof casserole dish on the stove over medium-high heat, add 2 tbsp olive oil and fry the beef in batches until browned all over. This will take about 15–20 minutes. Be careful not to overcrowd the pan as the meat will braise not brown.

Remove the beef to a deep plate. Replace the casserole dish on the stove, add another tbsp of oil, heat, then add the onion, leek and garlic. Fry for about 15 minutes over a low-medium heat until the onion is soft. (Once you add liquid, the onions will stop softening so it is important to take your time over this stage.)

Add the barley, stirring it through the onion, and cook for a few minutes.

Then add all the other vegetables, apart from the mushrooms, and fry with the onion for a couple of minutes. Put the beef back in the pot with the vegetables and pour over the wine and the stock. Add the herbs. Cover with a lid and cook over a low heat for about 1½ hours.

Fry the mushrooms in 1 dsp olive oil until soft, then add to the stew. Cook the stew for another 30 minutes.

Check the seasoning towards the end and add salt and black pepper to taste. Serve with either mashed potato or wide, flat pasta, such as pappardelle.

PORK, CHORIZO AND WHITE BEAN STEW

Tomato-y, intensely savoury, meaty, filling: this is one of those hero dishes that your friends and family will ask you to cook again and again. What you don't need to tell them is how uncomplicated it is to produce and, very pleasingly, just how inexpensive it is too. A kilo of outdoor-reared boneless pork shoulder will usually cost around £5, and this dish will feed six comfortably.

METHOD

Choose a pan that is large enough to eventually cook your stew – I use a sauteuse, a wide, shallow cross between a straight-sided frying pan and saucepan.

Pour a couple of tablespoons of oil into the pan over a medium heat, add the pork pieces in batches and fry for 10 minutes, or until browned on the outside but not completely cooked through, then remove from the pan.

Add the chorizo to the same pan and fry for 3–4 minutes. Remove from the pan and set aside with the pork.

Add the onion to the same pan and sweat over a low-medium heat for 10 minutes, until soft and translucent. Don't be tempted to hurry them: burnt onions are not nice. Add the garlic and cook for 2–3 minutes.

Pour in the wine and water and bring the mixture to a boil. Simmer for a few minutes before adding the sugar, chopped tomatoes, tomato purée and butter beans. Tip in the pork and chorizo. Bring the mixture to a gentle simmer over a low heat, place a lid over the pan and cook for 1 hour. Keep checking it to make sure that it doesn't catch, and add a little more water if the stew looks like it is becoming too dry.

Just before serving, check the seasoning and add salt and pepper to taste. I like to serve this in wide shallow bowls, sprinkled with the parsley, and over a big pile of mashed potato with buttered spring greens or kale on the side.

SERVES 6

olive oil, for frying
1kg boneless pork shoulder,
  cubed and rind removed
250g chorizo, chopped
1 large onion, chopped
2 garlic cloves, finely chopped
200ml white wine
200ml water
1 tbsp sugar
2 x 400g tins chopped tomatoes
squirt of tomato purée
200g tin butter beans, rinsed
  and drained
sea salt and freshly ground
  black pepper
4 tablespoons chopped
  flat-leaf parsley

PUFFED-UP BREAD PUDDING WITH CHEESE AND HAM

Do not be alarmed: I am not suggesting that you eat cheese and ham for dessert. It is merely that bread cooked in a savoury custard is traditionally referred to as a pudding, for reasons long lost. What this is, is a dish of bread cubes, cut from a white loaf – never pre-sliced – steeped in a mixture of milk and beaten egg, which causes it to rise beautifully in the oven, in the same manner as a Yorkshire pudding. (It is a kissing cousin to my Hot-Cross-Bun Bread-and-Butter Pudding on page 137). The cheese gives it a delectably crisp and crunchy topping, which contrasts with the fluffy, light interior.

The ham can either be slices torn into strips or, better still, cubes from a piece of meat.

You can serve this as a hearty one-dish supper, accompanied by a green salad with a sharp dressing to cut the richness, or use it as the starch to accompany a stew or a roast. It's also a clever dish to have up your sleeve as a winter vegetarian meal – omitting the ham, of course.

SERVES 6 AS A MAIN OR 8 AS A SIDE DISH

250g Cheddar
2 eggs
400ml milk
sea salt and freshly ground black pepper
butter, for greasing
275g white bread from a loaf (crusts removed), cut into 5cm cubes
100g ham, torn or cubed

SECRET
This isn't something you should cook in advance because it flops as it cools, making it look a lot less appealing.

METHOD

Preheat the oven to 180°C/350°F/gas mark 4.

Grate the Cheddar – if you are doing this in a food processor, use the smallest grating disc, as this helps the cheese melt more evenly, and go further.

Beat together the eggs and milk, adding a grind of black pepper and a pinch of salt (not too much because of the salty cheese), then add two-thirds of the cheese.

Butter a gratin dish liberally – this will give crisp, browned sides to your pudding – and arrange the bread cubes in it. They should be tumbled, as opposed to laid out in serried ranks, so that the top of the pudding is uneven. Sprinkle the ham over and between the bread cubes.

Pour over the egg mixture, making sure each bread cube is doused in the liquid. Then liberally scatter over the rest of the Cheddar.

Bake in the oven for 25–30 minutes, but resist the temptation to open the door during cooking as this will cause the pudding to deflate. It's ready when the top has browned and the pudding has puffed up. Serve immediately.

CHICKEN AND ROOT VEG TAGINE

I first made this Moroccan-inspired stew when I was snowed in with my mother a few years ago. We had woken up to find everything blanketed in virginal white. The snow kept coming down and the gritters hadn't been to our tiny village, so lunch was whatever I could come up with from the larder.

In weather like that, all I want to do is eat delicious, spicy food – central-heating for my soul. I found some chicken thighs in the freezer; and sweet potatoes, a butternut squash and an aging potato in the cupboard. I gathered up some olives and some blanched almonds, which ended up absorbing some of the lovely cooking juices and adding a great textural contrast to the meltingly soft vegetables. Served over some couscous, mixed with the seeds of a pomegranate that was lurking in the crisper drawer, it was the perfect winter lunch. Ten minutes' prep; forty minutes' bubbling with an occasional stir.

SERVES 6

6 chicken thighs with skin on (about 1kg)
flour, for dredging
2 tbsp olive oil
1 onion, finely chopped
1 tbsp Moroccan spicing (I use ras-el-hanout or berbere spice blend)
½ tsp ground cinnamon
1 medium sweet potato (300–350g), cut into large chunks
200g butternut squash, peeled and cut into large chunks
500g white potatoes, peeled and cut into large chunks
150g blanched almonds
1 large cup black and/or green olives (in my view, you can't have too many almonds or olives in a tagine, so add as many as you like)
200ml water
1 tbsp finely chopped, preserved lemon would be great, if you have it kicking around
couscous with pomegranate seeds and flaked almonds, to serve
chopped green herbs, to garnish

METHOD

Rinse the chicken thighs under the tap and pat dry with kitchen paper. Pour some flour into a shallow, wide bowl and dredge the chicken through it.

Heat the olive oil over a high heat in the wide frying pan in which the tagine will eventually be cooked. When the oil is popping, brown the chicken, 3 pieces at a time. (If added all at the same time it will reduce the cooking temperature of the oil, making the chicken soggy.) You are not cooking the chicken through, just browning it properly on all sides. This will take about 20 minutes. Once brown, remove the pan from the heat and place the chicken pieces on kitchen paper to drain.

When all the chicken has been browned, leave the fat in the pan, lower the heat to medium, tip in the chopped onion and cook slowly until it is translucent (about 10 minutes).

When the onion is cooked, add the Moroccan spices and cinnamon, and stir through the onion over the heat for 1 minute. Add the chicken pieces and ensure they are covered in the onion spice mixture. Add all the chopped vegetables, along with the almonds and olives.

Add the water and simmer for about 40 minutes until thickened and rich. Some of the potato chunks will break down, which will help to thicken the sauce. Add the preserved lemon, if using, 5 minutes before the end of the cooking time.

Serve with couscous. If you feel like it, add the pretty seeds of a pomegranate and some flaked almonds. Garnish the tagine and couscous with chopped fresh green herbs.

MINI MACARONI CHEESES

We ate a lot of macaroni cheese as children and I think it is now hard-wired into my brain as the ultimate comfort food. Whilst we often had variations – maybe Sunday's roast beef leftovers minced on Monday and layered over the pasta, or a layer of buttery, fried breadcrumbs added to the grated-cheese topping – it is the simple version to which I always return, seduced as I am by the silken,

smooth sauce; powerful cheese hit and tummy-filling goodness.

I've never really understood the approach that sees the traditional béchamel replaced by a mixture of cheeses – even, God forbid, cottage cheese. Use too much cheese and the mixture goes grainy, often separating to leave a film of orange oil on top of the pasta.

My special ingredient is Dijon mustard: the kick enhances the cheese flavour beautifully without it tasting, well, mustardy, and it helps thicken the sauce, too. I also find that it slightly lessens the amount of cheese that you need to use, as it adds so much rich flavour.

On that note, be careful not to over-thicken the sauce before you add the pasta, as the macaroni will absorb some of the liquid when it is flashed under the grill and you will end up with claggy macaroni cheese – the cardinal sin.

SERVES 6 (IT IS VERY RICH)
**250g Cheddar, plus 150g for
  the topping
350g macaroni
45g butter
50g plain flour
1 litre whole milk
3 tbsp Dijon mustard**

UTTERLY MOREISH CHEESES

Keen's farmhouse Cheddar *is a classic rich unpasteurised Cheddar from Somerset that is wonderful served as a big chunk surrounded by grapes and chutneys.*

Delicious crumbly unpasteurised **Pouligny-St-Pierre** *is an 'appellation d'origine contrôlée' triangular goat's cheese that looks great on a cheese board. It's the local cheese where I spend my summer holidays in France, and I've learnt to look for the green label packages – these are the 'fermier' (farmhouse) cheeses, as opposed to the red ('industriel').*

If I want to serve a single cheese, then I often choose the **Waterloo** *from Berkshire. It's mild, semi-soft, with a buttery flavour and made using a wash curd method.*

Its distinctive yellow colour is due to the natural carotene in the unpasteurised milk, which comes from a single herd of pedigree Guernsey cows near Henley.

If you love Brie, then it's worth seeking out the less common **Brie de Melun**. *It has a lovely, almost rippled-looking darker rind in contrast to the paler Brie de Meaux, and an almost salty tang to the creamy interior. Make friends with your local cheese shop so it's at the perfect point (not too runny) when you come to serve it.*

I have a thing for very creamy French cheese and one of my all-time favourites is **Saint-Félicien**. *A small-ish round, soft cheese, it's intensely rich, with a soft bloom to the rind. I often serve one of these alone for the cheese course if I'm just having three or four people for supper.*

METHOD

Grate the Cheddar for the sauce and for the topping, separately. I use the grating attachment on my food processor, but it can equally well be done by hand. (I keep bags of grated odds and ends of cheese in the freezer, and add them straight to the sauce without defrosting.)

Cook the macaroni in plenty of boiling water, according to the packet instructions – usually about 8 minutes. After the pasta is drained, pour over a kettle of boiling water to rinse off some of the starch, as this helps reduce the risk of unpleasant clagginess.

Meanwhile, melt the butter until it sizzles and sift in the flour – do sift, as it helps avoid lumps. Stir together rapidly, until a smooth paste is achieved. Then, start to add the milk. I like to start with about 150ml, just to get the sauce going. When that is mixed together, add about 250ml and whisk this together, being sure to scrape the corners of the pan, where the paste congregates. When it has started to thicken, add another big slosh of milk and vigorously whisk together.

Add the mustard, which you will find helps the thickening process, and whisk.

Continue until all the milk has been added. (I like to add the milk in increments as I find it thickens more quickly this way, and there is less likelihood of the sauce catching.)

Add the 250g cheese and beat into the sauce with a wooden spoon.

Turn on the grill to medium-high.

When the sauce is thick, but still slightly runny, tip in the pasta and stir carefully together.

You can either spoon this into one big dish, or in individual ones. I find it fills about 6 small pots.

Strew the cheese for the topping over the pasta. Place under the grill for about 5–10 minutes, until the top is golden and bubbling. Do keep an eye on it, as it can burn in an instant.

Serve with a green salad or some sliced tomatoes.

GRATED POTATO GRATIN

This is very good hot as a main course (leave out the ham for an excellent vegetarian option) and served with a green salad. It also works well as a substantial side dish served with roast chicken or pork chops, and is equally good cold as hot – we used to take chunks of it in our school lunchboxes. It reheats like a dream, both in the oven and microwave.

The recipe is adapted from the 1971 cookbook, *Poor Cook*, by Caroline Conran and Susan Campbell, from which much of my mother's kitchen repertoire came. It is one of the first things I learnt to cook, and was a foolproof standby that served me well all through university in Newcastle where, in winter, an icy wind whips over the city from the North Sea and food that can be used as internal central-heating is essential.

SERVES 6 AS A MAIN OR 8 AS A SIDE DISH

1 tbsp softened butter, plus extra for greasing and topping
500g potatoes
1 tbsp olive oil
½ large onion, chopped
1 garlic clove, crushed
50g ham, cut into thin strips about 2.5cm long (optional)
2 eggs
25g Parmesan, grated
100g Gruyère or Cheddar, grated
275ml whole milk
couple of grinds black pepper
pinch of grated nutmeg

SECRET
The best potatoes for this dish are Maris Pipers.

METHOD
Preheat the oven to 180°C/350°F/gas mark 4. Use a piece of kitchen paper and a little butter to grease a gratin dish.

Peel the potatoes and grate them. This can be done with a box grater, but it is the work of moments (and runs less risk of grating your fingertips) if you use the grating attachment on a food processor, which I highly recommend.

Tip the grated potatoes into a bowl, and then squeeze out all the starchy liquid with your hands over the kitchen sink. However, it is important not to rinse the potatoes at any point, as you need some starch to thicken the dish. (You will be amazed at how much liquid comes off the potatoes.)

Add the olive oil and butter to a frying pan over a low-medium heat and, when the butter has melted, fry the onion and garlic for about 10 minutes, being careful not to brown then. Add the ham, if using.

In a large mixing bowl beat together the eggs, Parmesan, half the Gruyère or Cheddar, plus the milk, black pepper and nutmeg.

Add the cooked onions to the grated potatoes and mix together. Tip everything into the buttered gratin dish, then pour over the eggy cheese mixture. Flatten the top of the potatoes and dot the top with the butter. Strew the remaining grated cheese over the dish.

Bake in the oven for approximately 45 minutes. Depending on the depth and heat of the oven this can take from 35–60 minutes, so do keep an eye on it. If the top is browning too quickly, loosely cover it with a piece of foil.

GRANNY HORSE'S CROSS-HATCHED POTATOES

This dish has always been known as Granny Horse's Potatoes: I've never seen potatoes cooked in this way elsewhere and, every time I eat them, I am transported back to her tiny cottage, filled with equestrian memorabilia, in the beautiful village of Avon Bassett in Warwickshire. That's Granny Horse in the photo on the right.

My grandparents had the luxury of a huge garden. Granny ended up in charge of the flowers and Grandpa was very much in charge of vegetables, which he grouped in serried ranks. Peas, beans, lettuces, leeks, parsnips, cabbages and, of course, potatoes all made their way straight from the soil to the kitchen.

This way of cooking potatoes, which Granny showed me, really pays homage to the taste of a great potato, because they are good enough to eat on their own. The edges caramelise in the heat of the oven and they are simultaneously fluffy, crispy and chewy. Please don't be scared by the amount of butter: think about the amount you'd put on a baked potato. Do not substitute margarine or oil, as the potatoes will not crisp.

SERVES 4 (I USUALLY COUNT ON 3 HALVES PER PERSON)

6 large potatoes
150g softened butter
sea salt and freshly ground
  black pepper

METHOD

Preheat the oven to 180°C/350°F/gas mark 4. Halve the potatoes lengthways and score them about 1.2cm deep, in a criss-cross pattern, with three strokes in each direction. Spread butter thickly over the surface – the liquid content of the potatoes can make the butter slide, but persevere.

Sprinkle a generous amount of salt and black pepper over each half and bake for about 45 minutes until golden and cooked through.

> ## SECRET
> A floury potato is what's best here – it really doesn't work with new or waxy potatoes, so I recommend King Edwards, Maris Pipers or generic baking potatoes.

SALADS AND FOOD FOR HOT SUMMER DAYS

Salads are, hands down, the most popular recipes that I write on my blog. Usually they are a result of pulling out whatever is lurking in the fridge and adding whatever looked good at the greengrocer's that day. I think it's that ease that appeals: most of them take minutes to assemble, yet feel like so much more than the sum of their parts.

I always think it's cheating a bit to call a salad a 'recipe', when mostly it's just a case of combining a few ingredients; this means that the secret of a successful dish is in the things you choose to mix together. A good rule of thumb is always to include a protein (cheese, pulses, meat) and a fruit (tomato, avocado, cucumber, pomegranate seeds), with something leafy, and maybe some seeds or nuts.

I also think it's important not to be worried about measures or finding the exact same ingredients. A little more or less of anything rarely hurts a salad and often substitutions can be inspired. That being said, it's probably best not to play around too much with the proportions of a salad dressing, as the mixture of flavours is usually calibrated with thought.

If you have room, it's worth collecting some interesting oils and vinegars and playing around with dressing ideas. I have walnut oil, hazelnut oil, avocado oil and an excellent single-estate rapeseed oil; plus, a proper, aged and sticky balsamic vinegar, white wine vinegar and sherry vinegar. Good mustards are also a great way to perk up a salad. Try wholegrain, or one that is infused with herbs or spices.

LIBERTYLONDONGIRL'S SALAD

This is one of the most popular recipes I have ever written. I must admit to a slight astonishment, given its simplicity, but then again it is the salad that I eat all year round with a few variations, and I reckon it comes in at under 15 minutes from fridge to mouth. It's wonderful in winter because the crunch of the onion and the sharp tang of the lemon juice con your senses into believing that spring could be just around the corner.

   Best of all, it has just four main ingredients. Of course, you could substitute pretty much any kind of cheese for the halloumi, but do think about the contrast of textures. A vegan reader once asked about substituting marinated tofu in this recipe, and I don't see why not, as long as it is firm or pressed tofu.

   Do not make this salad in advance, as the avocado goes mushy.

SERVES 4

1 red onion
1 avocado
400g tin chickpeas,
   drained and rinsed
good squeeze of fresh lemon
   juice
lemon zest (optional)
250g halloumi
sea salt and freshly ground
   black pepper
dash of good olive oil
   (preferably the herby, grassy
   Greek stuff)
1 tbsp chopped flat-leaf parsley
lettuce leaves and toasted pitta
   bread, to serve

METHOD

Finely chop the red onion by making vertical slices, and then cutting across before chopping some more.

Roughly dice the flesh of the avocado and mix it with the chickpeas and onion, adding the lemon juice and some zest, if you like. Hands are good for this.

Cut the halloumi into slices about 0.5cm thick, then place in a hot frying pan (a griddle pan if you have one) without any oil, until it is browned on each side. Chop it up into small bite-size pieces. (I always cook more than I need for the salad as I tend to eat quite a lot en route ...)

Add the halloumi to the rest of the ingredients, along with salt, black pepper, the olive oil and parsley. Mix together well.

Serve with lettuce leaves (Cos or little gem, for the crunch), and pitta bread, for scooping.

GREEN LENTILS AND GOAT'S CHEESE WITH MUSTARD DRESSING

I used to make this for lunch for my roommate, Jackie, and me on those summer days in Manhattan's East Village when the heat seemed to shiver in the air above the pavement, and spending any time at all in our un-airconditioned apartment kitchen felt like a trial. Sitting on the tiny fire escape, eating this from mismatched and chipped bowls, five floors up from the street, we watched New Yorkers briskly walking down the block, seemingly unaffected by the heat.

The creamy cheese, earthy lentils, peppery watercress and piquant mustard really are one of those great salad combinations.

SERVES 4 FOR LUNCH
OR 6 FOR A FIRST COURSE
250g Puy or green lentils
150g quinoa
125g cubed goat's cheese
   (I like the kind that comes in
   a fat, round slice with a
   cloudy white rind)
1 tbsp chopped flat-leaf parsley
sea salt and freshly ground
   black pepper
generous handful watercress
2 little gem lettuces

For the dressing
1 tsp Dijon mustard
1 tbsp olive oil
dash of lemon juice or
   balsamic vinegar

METHOD
Put 2 saucepans of water on to boil.

Cook the lentils and quinoa separately in lots of simmering water according to the packet instructions. Whilst they are cooking, make the dressing. Put the mustard, olive oil and lemon juice or balsamic vinegar in a bowl and whisk well (or put in a jar and shake).

When the lentils and quinoa are cooked, drain them and rinse briefly. Add to a large bowl with the dressing and mix in. Add the goat's cheese and parsley, and season with salt and black pepper. Serve with the watercress and lettuce.

BUFFALO MOZZARELLA WITH BLOOD ORANGES

In cold, dark January when the nights seem longer than the days, the arrival of the blood oranges from Italy and Spain give a promise of summer ahead. Streaked with dark red in both flesh and peel, they give a subtle hint of raspberry along with their citrus tang.

In this salad, they make a delicious contrast to the salty olives and cheese, which is balanced by the crisp lettuce.

You do need to remove the pith and membrane from the orange pieces, but learning to supreme an orange is a very handy skill, although you may destroy a few before you get the knack. First take a very sharp, small knife and slice the top and bottom of the fruit across, taking care not to cut too deep. Then slice all the peel, pith and membrane from the fruit, top to bottom, revealing the fruit underneath. Slip the knife along each vertical segment to remove each slice with no pith or membrane attached.

SERVES 4 AS A STARTER
2 buffalo mozzarella cheeses
2 blood oranges
1 head of romaine lettuce
50g black olives, pitted
olive oil
sea salt and freshly ground
  black pepper

METHOD
Drain the mozzarella and pat dry with kitchen paper. Then tear the mozzarella into small pieces. (Do not cut it.)

Supreme the oranges (see introduction, above) and pull each supreme of orange in half.

Remove the outer leaves of the lettuce and discard (or make the Lettuce Soup from page 103). Slice the lettuce across into 1cm pieces.

Cut the olives in half lengthways.

Divide the ingredients between 4 plates and drizzle over a little olive oil. Season with salt and black pepper.

Orange-Scented Fragrances for a Perpetual Summer

I always wear a citrus fragrance – preferably one with orange-blossom notes – and these are some of the tried-and-tested favourites that I always have in my home.

Fragonard Fleur d'Oranger Eau de Toilette

Diptyque Fresh Lotion for the Body

Le Labo Neroli 36 Perfume Oil

Tom Ford Neroli Portofino Eau de Parfum

Jo Malone Orange Blossom Cologne

Malin+Goetz Neroli Candle

Molton Brown Orange & Bergamot Body Wash

SOBA, PEANUT AND TOFU SALAD

Although this is Japanese in origin, it always reminds me of St Mawes in Cornwall, where my friend, Hannah, first made it for our lunch when we were on holiday one summer. I was unenthusiastic at the prospect, but she had control of the stove and I do try not to take over every kitchen into which I walk ... At my first mouthful I felt rather stupid, as it was a revelation. I never thought cold noodles could taste this good: the crunch of the pepper with the sharpness of the dressing, the yielding quality of the tofu and the slippery noodles make this a strangely addictive dish.

SERVES 4

200g soba noodles
1 carrot
bunch spring onions
1 red pepper
200g firm tofu
handful coriander or mint
  leaves, finely chopped

For the dressing
125g crunchy peanut butter
handful roasted unsalted
  peanuts, finely chopped
1 tbsp rice vinegar
juice of ½ lime
1 garlic clove, crushed
1cm piece ginger, grated
1 tbsp honey or agave nectar
2 tbsp soy sauce

METHOD

Cook the noodles according to the packet instructions, then refresh in cold water. Drain well.

Grate the carrot and slice the spring onions, pepper and tofu in slivers or matchsticks.

Combine all the dressing ingredients in a large bowl and add all the chopped vegetables and the tofu. Then carefully toss in the noodles and herbs, ensuring they are all covered in dressing.

STYLISH AND DELICIOUS PLACES TO REST YOUR FEET IN DEPARTMENT STORES

BG IN BERGDORF GOODMAN (NEW YORK)

On the seventh floor of Bergdorf Goodman, this pale-blue sanctuary designed by cult decorator Kelly Wearstler, with its ravishing view over Central Park, is the spiritual home of Manhattan ladies-who-lunch. But, fear not, there is more than salad and tuna tartare to eat here: the lobster mac 'n' cheese is artery-sticking-ly good and the croque monsieur a gourmand's delight.

5th Avenue at 58th Street, New York, NY 10019; www.bergdorfgoodman.com

ROSE BAKERY AT DOVER STREET MARKET (LONDON, NEW YORK AND TOKYO)

Paris's lovely Rose Bakery has expanded internationally under the aegis of possibly the world's most directional fashion superstore with its cult assiette de légumes, and delicious baked goods (the carrot cake is particularly noteworthy), providing a down-to-earth counterpoint to the often extraordinary clothes on sale next door. Warning: they often sell out of savoury food before 4pm, so do arrive early.

www.doverstreetmarket.com

PRIMO PIANO AT LE BON MARCHÉ (PARIS)

On the Left Bank in Saint-Germain-des-Prés, the venerable Bon Marché hides a wonderful secret – Primo Piano, with its adjacent outdoor, tree-shaded courtyard serving good Italian food, as well as tartines and a killer cheesecake.

Le Bon Marché, 24 Rue de Sèvres, 75007 Paris; www.primo-piano.fr

THREE BRILLIANT BOOKSHOPS FOR COOKS IN NEW YORK

1. JOANNE HENDRICKS

Not far from my old Manhattan apartment, this wonderful bookshop also sells all manner of culinary ephemera, including menus, prints, photographs, cookware and etiquette guides, in addition to a glorious assortment of rare food books. If you are looking for a particular first edition, this is the place to ask.

488 Greenwich Street, New York, NY 10013; www.joannehendrickscookbooks.com

2. STRAND BOOKSTORE

Because the Strand buys thousands of books every day, including secondhand, and has the largest rare books collection in New York City, they have a phenomenal cookbook department with plenty of treasures by long-forgotten cookbook writers to be unearthed. They also have great discounts on list prices (often cheaper than Amazon).

828 Broadway, New York, NY 10003–4805; www.strandbooks.com

3. KITCHEN ARTS & LETTERS

With over 13,000 titles in stock (domestic and imported, contemporary and out of print), this not-very-big shop in the upper reaches of the Upper East Side has an influence far beyond its size. Do sign up to its brilliant newsletters.

1435 Lexington Avenue, New York, NY 10128; www.kitchenartsandletters.com

AND ONE IN LONDON ...

BOOKS FOR COOKS

This Notting-Hill-based shop is legendary amongst UK food lovers. Their café tests recipes from the cookbooks and cookery classes take place in the demonstration kitchen upstairs. I also highly recommend curling up in their delightfully squashy sofa to test-read the books.

4 Blenheim Crescent, Notting Hill, London W11 1NN; www.booksforcooks.com

KALE WITH WALNUT DRESSING

Whenever I am in Los Angeles, it can seem as though no one there eats anything but kale. Steamed, raw, chipped: it is on every menu. And with good reason. Kale is a superfood, packed with nutrients. Don't be put off by serving it raw: just make sure you chop it very fine to minimise the necessary chewing.

SERVES 4
50g walnuts
30ml walnut oil
1 tsp sherry vinegar
45g plain yogurt
sea salt and freshly ground black pepper
250g kale

METHOD
Roughly chop the walnuts and place in a frying pan over a medium-high heat for about 5 minutes, until they are lightly toasted.

Set aside 1 tbsp walnuts and place the remainder in a food processor with all the other ingredients, except for the kale. Pulse until the nuts are quite small. Taste and season to your liking. (This is quite a sharp dressing, but it does work very well against the kale.)

Run a sharp knife down each side of the kale stems to remove them, then roll each leaf half into a sausage and slice very thinly. This will give fine strips of kale.

Heap the kale into a serving dish, pour over the dressing and mix through. Sprinkle over the reserved, chopped walnuts.

CUCUMBER AND SESAME SALAD

This is a simple and refreshing salad that clears the palate. Perfect on a hot summer day. (See photograph on page 61.)

SERVES 4 AS A SIDE DISH
1 cucumber
2 tbsp white sesame seeds

For the vinaigrette
1 tbsp groundnut oil
1 dsp sesame oil
1 dsp rice vinegar
1 dsp mirin or Chinese rice wine
pinch of caster sugar

METHOD
Peel the cucumber and slice it thinly, either with a very sharp knife, or using a mandoline on its middle setting.

Arrange the cucumber on a serving dish. Whisk together the vinaigrette ingredients and pour over the cucumber. Scatter the sesame seeds over the top just before serving.

AVOCADO, GRAPEFRUIT AND RED ONION SALAD

This is a salad that divides opinion, but I think the creaminess of the avocado and the crunch and tang of the onion, paired with the sharp, citrus hit of the grapefruit, is a wonderful combination.

I first made it in New Jersey with a big, fat, Florida pink grapefruit and a couple of perfect avocados I had bought in Delicious Orchards, one of my favourite NJ fresh-produce markets. (I love it for the name, as much as anything).

As well as a quick, light lunch, this is a perfect first course, too, as it gets the taste buds going.

SERVES 4
1 large pink grapefruit
1 red onion
2 avocados
1 round, soft lettuce (such as Webbs)

For the dressing
squeeze of lime juice
2 tbsp good olive oil
1 tsp Dijon mustard (optional)
sea salt and freshly ground black pepper

METHOD
To supreme the grapefruit, using a very sharp knife, slice the peel and pith off the grapefruit and release the segments from the tough membranes. I don't like big segments in my salads, as I find them too overpowering – better to break them up if they are very big. For the same reason, slice across the red onion into rings as fine as you can get them. Then halve them.

Peel and slice the avocados as thinly as possible, then cut each slice into pieces. Roughly chop the lettuce. Put the lettuce in a serving bowl and arrange the avocados, grapefruit and onion on top.

Combine all the ingredients for the dressing (I like to shake them together in a jam jar) and drizzle over the salad.

GRILLED COURGETTES WITH LICKABLE DRESSING

Every day in the middle of the annual August courgette glut, I see pleas on Twitter from people wanting recipes to use them up, before they bolt and turn into marrows with rhino-thick skin. My two favourite ways to cook them are either grated and stir-fried, then mixed into pasta or noodles, or grilled – as they are here.

I ring the changes with dressings, but I made this simple yogurt one for my oldest schoolfriend, Clare, one night, and I caught her licking her plate, so it has fans other than me.

SERVES 1
1 courgette
olive oil

For the dressing
2 dsp plain yogurt
sea salt and freshly ground black pepper
3 mint sprigs, leaves finely chopped

METHOD
Chop the courgette lengthways into thick slices. Slick them with olive oil and place into a preheated, ridged, cast-iron grill pan on top of the stove. Resisting the temptation to keep prodding them, leave them for about 3–4 minutes each side, before turning them onto a plate.

For the dressing, thin the yogurt with water to a pouring consistency and season with salt and black pepper. Pour onto the courgettes and top with the mint.

To go with this, I usually make a salad with soft lettuce leaves: a little gem; skinned cucumber chunks; a handful of chopped, green beans zapped in a puddle of water in the microwave for 2 minutes and refreshed under the cold tap; and a couple of celery sticks, chopped.

Over it all, I sprinkle some good olive oil and sometimes pumpkin, sunflower and sesame seeds.

MIDWINTER SALAD WITH ROASTED CAULIFLOWER, MAPLE WALNUTS AND POMEGRANATE

This is for a wintry day when you despair of ever having a full day of sunlight. The sweet-sour flavours and the crunch of the seeds and walnuts make this quite addictive. I first made it for a supper party I threw at my London flat for a group of fashion editors and they inhaled it.

There are quite a few processes to get through in this salad, but it helps that they can all be done in advance (even the night before), although I do think that the cauliflower is much nicer roasted just before you need it, so that it is pleasantly warm in the salad, rather than cold.

SERVES 6–8
1 large cauliflower
2 tbsp olive or rapeseed oil
sea salt and freshly ground
   black pepper
1 tbsp maple syrup
1 tbsp light muscovado sugar
75g walnuts, very roughly
   chopped
½ pomegranate
bag of watercress

For the dressing
2 tbsp tahini
½ tbsp pomegranate molasses
2 tbsp olive oil
generous pinch of sea salt
2 tsp fresh lemon juice

METHOD
Preheat the oven to 200°C/400°F/gas mark 6.

Divide the cauliflower into florets and then break into smaller pieces. Put in a roasting tin and toss with the olive or rapeseed oil and some salt and pepper. Roast for about 30 minutes, until the cauliflower is browned – almost charred – in places.

In a small bowl, mix together the maple syrup and muscovado sugar, and add the walnuts. Mix with your hands, then tip out into a non-stick frying pan over a high heat and toast for about 10 minutes, stirring frequently, until they caramelise. Keep an eye on them so that they do not catch and burn.

Hold the pomegranate half over a bowl and bash the back with a wooden spoon. Miraculously the seeds will pop out. Pick over them, removing any bits of white pith.

Make the dressing by mixing together all the ingredients.

Place some watercress on each plate and then divide the cauliflower, pomegranate seeds and walnuts between each one. Drizzle over the dressing using a spoon.

FASHION MUSEUMS I LOVE

UK: Fashion Museum at Bath Assembly Rooms

Every year a guest curator picks a dress of the year. They are all on display and make a wonderful cultural history of fashion dating back to 1963. There is also a lovely selection of dressing-up costumes for children.

Bennett Street, Bath, Somerset BA1 2QH; www.nationaltrust.org.uk/bath-assembly-rooms

UK: Fashion Collection at the V&A, London

Spanning four centuries, the V&A's Fashion Collection is the largest and most comprehensive collection of dress in the world. (I'm pleased to note that my aunt has a pair of shoes in there.) Do keep an eye out for the regular special exhibitions.

Cromwell Road, London SW7 2RL; www.vam.ac.uk

UK: Dress and Fashion Collection at The Museum of London

I love wandering around the Galleries of Modern London here, as the clothes are displayed contextually, so you can see their cultural relevance. There are around 60 complete outfits and more than 200 accessories dating from the late sixteenth century to the present day.

150 London Wall, London EC2Y 5HN, www.museumoflondon.org.uk

UK: The Fan Museum, Greenwich, London

The fan museum – in two grade II-listed houses built in 1721, within the Greenwich World Heritage Site – is home to more than 4,000 predominantly antique fans from around the world, dating from the eleventh century to the present day. As a bonus, it has a wonderful tea room.

12 Crooms Hill, London SE10 8ER; www.thefanmuseum.org.uk

UK: Gallery of Costume at Manchester Art Gallery

The Gallery of Costume is housed in the elegant Platt Hall, an eighteenth-century textile merchant's home, and contains over 20,000 items from the seventeenth century to the present day.

Platt Hall, Rusholme, Manchester M14 5LL; www.manchestergalleries.org

France: Les Arts Décoratifs, Paris

Part of the Louvre buildings, Les Arts Décoratifs is actually four collections, amongst which is Mode et Textile. Whilst the permanent collection here is for scholars, the temporary exhibitions it puts on – from the history of underwear to a Hussein Chalayan retrospective – are always fascinating, beautiful, and make a welcome break from the lure of the Parisian shops.

107 Rue de Rivoli, 75001 Paris; www.lesartsdecoratifs.fr

US: The Museum at FIT (Fashion Institute of Technology), New York

I would spend hours here when I lived in New York: quite apart from its spectacular temporary shows, the Fashion and Textile History Gallery changes its exhibits very six months, pulling pieces from its permanent collection of over 50,000 garments and accessories from the eighteenth century to the present day.

227 West 27th St, New York, NY 10001; www.fitnyc.edu

US: Costume Institute at the Metropolitan Museum of Art, New York

Its yearly fashion exhibition grabs headlines worldwide, thanks to Anna Wintour's ceaseless championing of its cause and, whilst some of the previous concepts seem a little tenuous (Superheroes: Fashion and Fantasy springs to mind), shows like the recent Alexander McQueen Savage Beauty were unmissable.

1000 Fifth Avenue, New York, New York 10028-0198; www.metmuseum.org

HALLOUMI AND PERSIMMON SALAD

My very first memory of persimmons is seeing them on a large, flat tray in long-closed Greek-Cypriot restaurant, Milou's Kebab House, on Charlotte Street in London's Fitzrovia – a place I was first brought to in my carrycot. I must have been around seven or eight, and I remember asking my mother what they could possibly be. They are bright orange, sized somewhere between a plum and a nectarine, with the smooth, slightly shiny skin of both, but with a coronet (known as the pistil) of leaves on top. Sliced into, they are fleshy with no visible seeds. Taste-wise, they are very, very sweet.

In recent years, they've become much more common. Every time I see them, I get to thinking about salt and sweet together – a taste combination I've only ever liked in retro cheese-and-pineapple sticks. I wondered what would happen with very salty halloumi cheese against the super-sweet persimmons. I now know that it works brilliantly: I added a trickle of reduced balsamic vinegar and the acid enhanced the salt-sweet combination perfectly.

This would make a wonderful Christmas Day starter. The combination of taste-bud-accelerating ingredients would be perfect before the creamy, carby richness of the main course. You can slice the cheese in advance and reduce the balsamic, but do not slice the persimmons before you need them as they will brown and go woolly.

There are no precise quantities for this. Allow one persimmon per person, sliced across, not down, so that you get a pretty star effect in the middle of each slice; and and use the same number and width of halloumi slices. Heat the cheese in a hot griddle pan (with no oil), if you have one – a frying pan will do – until it is browned on each side.

Pour a few tablespoons of balsamic vinegar into a saucepan and heat gently until reduced to a thick syrup. (It only takes a minute or two, so keep an eye on it, otherwise it sticks like glue to the pan.)

Then layer the pretty orange and cream slices together. Sprinkle over sea salt and some black pepper. You could serve it with watercress or a little bit of chopped mint, but it's just as good served plain, on its own.

KOHLRABI REMOULADE (SORT OF)

This is my modern play on a traditional remoulade dressing, which is most often a mustard-flavoured mayonnaise, usually seen in France coating grated, raw celeriac.

I only started eating kohlrabi last year: I had seen the pastel-green and slightly shiny bulbs, with their alien tentacles, on my local market stall but had no idea what to do with them. It didn't help either that my dear French friend, Yoann, refers to them as 'food for ze cattle'.

When one arrived in my weekly farm vegetable box, looking like it had just landed from a sci-fi props store, I stared at it for a while, then sliced a bit off. And blow me down if it didn't taste, not like the earthy root I was expecting, but rather like a raw broccoli stalk. Delicious. I didn't want to cook it, so I thought that a riff on the creamy remoulade dressing would complement that green, fresh crunch. You can make this a little in advance as the lemon juice stops the kohlrabi discolouring.

Do try it: it's now one of my favourite quick salads.

SERVES 6 AS A SIDE SALAD

1kg kohlrabi (about 5 small bulbs)
2 tsp Sriracha chilli sauce (add more if you like a kick)
6 tbsp mayonnaise
2 tsp lemon juice
sea salt and freshly ground black pepper

METHOD

Peel off the outside of each kohlrabi with a vegetable peeler and lop off the tentacles with a paring knife.

Grate the kohlrabi using either a box grater or the standard grating attachment on a food processor. (Do be careful not to use the ultrafine grating attachment as this makes the kohrabi too fine and watery.)

Mix the chilli sauce into the mayonnaise, along with the lemon juice. Add the kohlrabi and mix through the dressing.

Taste and season with salt and black pepper.

GRILLED PEPPERS WITH PRESERVED LEMON, PINE NUTS AND MINT

Inspired both by a trip I took to Marrakesh with my sister, and by one of my mother's failsafe starters, this classic dish of peppers is perked up by the salty mouth-pucker of the lemons, whilst the mint adds a lovely, fresh note.

SERVES 4

8 red, sweet, pointed Romano
   peppers
25g pine nuts
2 tbsp good olive oil
1 preserved lemon, to taste
3 large sprigs of mint, leaves
   roughly chopped, plus extra
   whole leaves to garnish
sea salt and freshly ground
   black pepper
pitta bread, olives, radishes
   and capers, to serve

METHOD

Preheat the grill to high, then place the peppers on a rack and grill for 7–10 minutes, until they are blistered and blackened. Turn them over with tongs and grill the undersides, too. Put the peppers in a large, plastic food bag, seal and set aside for 10 minutes – this makes the skins easier to remove.

Meanwhile, toast the pine nuts in a frying pan until golden. Transfer to a plate and set aside.

Remove the skins and stalks from the peppers and discard both, then cut the peppers in half lengthways and remove the seeds and membrane. Cut the peppers into long strips and transfer to a large bowl, along with any cooking juices from the bag. Pour over the olive oil.

Halve and deseed the preserved lemon, finely slice, then add to the bowl of peppers along with the chopped mint leaves. Season with salt and black pepper. Set aside for an hour or two, allowing the flavours to mix.

To serve, remove the peppers and lemons from the bowl using tongs and arrange on a serving platter. Pour over the oil from the marinade, sprinkle with the toasted pine nuts and garnish with the whole mint leaves. Serve with warm pitta bread and little dishes of olives, radishes and capers.

ROASTED CHERRY TOMATO AND SWEETCORN SALAD

I always adored succotash when I lived in America. Before I landed, I'd read about it in novels, but really had no idea what it actually was until I was fed it at Thanksgiving one year. For those of you who also have no idea, it's a dish of stewed corn kernels and lima beans, cooked with chopped tomatoes and onions, served warm. That was the inspiration for this dish. There are no lima beans and no stewing, but the basic premise of fresh corn and tomatoes remains the same.

SERVES 6 AS A SIDE DISH
1kg cherry tomatoes
decent slug of Greek olive oil
sprinkling of coarse sea salt
lots of black pepper
fresh, torn basil
4 corn cobs or 250g tinned
sweetcorn

METHOD
Preheat the oven to 150°C/300°F/gas mark 2.

Place the tomatoes, olive oil, salt, black pepper and some torn basil in a roasting tin and put in the oven to roast.

While they are cooking, slice the corn kernels vertically off the cob using a sharp knife. (I learnt to do this in New Jersey: it's not a usual way of preparing corn in the UK, where it's pretty much always served on the cob, or bought in kernels either sold in a can or frozen.)

Roast the tomatoes for about 30–40 minutes until really soft and slightly caramelised around the edges. They will give off lots of liquid. Leave the oven on.

Remove the tomatoes from the tin, leaving behing the juices, and set aside. Tip in the corn kernels into the roasting tin and return to the oven for about 15 minutes so that the flavours can mingle, and the corn soften a little.

Pour the tomatoes, corn and juices into a serving bowl and add more basil to serve.

SECRET
If you can buy your corn cobs at a market, ask to taste the kernels. They should be sweet, plump and fresh. If they are at all chewy, dry or bland then used tinned sweetcorn.

KITCHEN SUPPERS

I've been lucky enough to have had a large dining table to fit my friends around in my London apartments but, when I lived in Manhattan, I had a tiny, galley kitchen and a doll's-house-sized table. I didn't let that stop me from having people round to eat, though: four people squeezed at the table and me at the stove made for many happy evenings. (Not least because I was one of the very few people in my circle that ever cooked. That New York cliché about storing sweaters in ovens is a cliché for a reason.)

I just cannot imagine not cooking supper for my friends and family, wherever I find myself. Whether it's in my friend Julian's crazy band house in Los Angeles' Koreatown, where I served up late-night Indian meals to the boys after rehearsal; or in Ibiza after a long weekend of dancing, when it's all about outdoor feasts of restorative salads, gathering up everyone around a table for a relaxed meal is one of the loveliest ways to spend time with friends.

In London I cook supper at least twice a week for a motley crew: I invite whoever is around to join me and I cook simple meals that don't require me to stop work early, or spend hours chopping.

This chapter is the cumulative result of cooking for my friends around the world, with whatever came to hand at the time. There are recipes I've nicked from my mother — and grandmother. There are things I like to eat when I'm on my own (a kitchen supper can just as easily be for me and the sausage dog as for the five thousand), and dishes friends ask for again and again. Above all, they are uncomplicated and delicious.

MUSHROOM LASAGNE

There's very little I dislike more than a parsimonious vegetarian lasagne, redolent of school dinners, filled with lumps of watery vegetables, metallic tomato sauce, a white sauce that has been all but sucked up by the pasta and topped with a few cheese scrapings. If you're going to bother with lasagne, it should be thick, luxurious and wholly satisfying. There are three or four different versions in my arsenal but my absolute favourite is this mushroom one, using lots of different types of mushroom. (There will be no watery courgettes, inappropriate root vegetables, pappy aubergines or insufficiently cooked-down tomatoes on my watch.)

SERVES 8

1 quantity Slow-Cooked Tomato Sauce (see page 82 and made using only chopped and cherry tomatoes)

1.5kg mushrooms (I like mixed flat, white and chestnut)

50g butter

3 tbsp olive oil

approx. 10–14 lasagna sheets

For the cheese sauce

50g butter

50g plain flour, sifted

500ml whole milk

2 tbsp Dijon mustard

250g Cheddar, finely grated

For the topping

150g Cheddar, finely grated

100g fried breadcrumbs (to make your own, see method on page 75), or panko breadcrumbs (optional)

METHOD

Make the Slow-Cooked Tomato Sauce first so that it is happily simmering away (for a minimum of 45 minutes) while you get on with the rest.

Slice the mushrooms into thirds, then across into cubes. Put a large frying pan over the heat with the butter and oil and, when the butter has melted, tip in the mushrooms. Don't let them cook too quickly: the trick is soften the mushrooms without them losing their plumpness. When they are cooked, take off the heat and put to one side.

For the cheese sauce, melt the butter in a large, heavy-bottomed pan (this is to stop your sauce burning) and beat in the sifted flour.

Add a ladleful of milk and whisk in. As it thickens, carefully add in another measure of milk, and so on. Add in the mustard and the Cheddar and beat together with a wooden spoon until the Cheddar melts. When the sauce has thickened enough that it coats the back of a spoon without falling off, take it off the heat.

Preheat the oven to 180°C/350°F/gas mark 4.

Pour a ladleful of cheese sauce over the entire bottom of a large gratin dish. Then add the first layer of lasagna sheets. (You may need to break some to ensure they fit neatly.)

Over this add a thin layer of tomato sauce. Then a layer of mushrooms, followed by a layer of cheese sauce. Next: a layer of lasagna. (Try to keep the layers as thin as possible.) Repeat until the dish is almost, but not quite, full. Make sure that the topmost layer is lasagna sheets spread with a little cheese sauce.

For the topping, strew over the Cheddar, then the fried breadcrumbs, if using. Bake in the oven for about 35–45 minutes.

INDIVIDUAL CHICKEN POT PIES

Pie. **There's** a word to strike joy in the heart. Really, who doesn't like pie? There is rarely a situation where you can't serve a pie. I always serve Giant Chicken Pies at my annual birthday cocktail party (see page 173), and a fruit pie makes a perfect Sunday-lunch pudding.

I also like little pies, which are great for supper parties. They are easier to manoeuvre and, if you are having a slightly smarter meal or, equally, one where there is already lots on the table with no room for a big dish, then everyone can be served a neat plate, with accompaniments. **The enamel dishes I use have a diameter of 10cm at the base and 12cm across the top**, but narrower and deeper dishes would work just as well.

These individual chicken and leek pot pies are one of my go-to recipes when I am having a work dinner at home. (I've yet to find a fashion editor who can resist these, pastry included.)

Ah, yes. The pastry. I make no apology for using ready-rolled all-butter puff pastry in these little pies. Shop-bought pastry takes away all the stress, leaving you to concentrate on making the delicious, creamy middle.

I make the filling from scratch, which appeals to the thrifty side of my nature, as you will be left with lots of lovely chicken stock for soup afterwards.

MAKES 8 SMALL PIES
For the poached chicken
1 large, organic, free-range chicken, or 4 thighs and 4 leg pieces (around 1.2–1.5kg)
1 carrot
1 onion
1 leek

For the pie
100g butter, plus extra for frying
sea salt and freshly ground black pepper
1 tbsp Dijon mustard
1 litre chicken stock (see Method)
2 leeks
100g plain flour, plus extra for dusting
1kg ready-made puff pastry
2 eggs, lightly beaten
8 mini pie dishes

METHOD

For the poached chicken, rinse the chicken under the cold tap and place it in a deep saucepan. Roughly chop the vegetables and add to the pan. Cover the chicken with cold water and bring to the boil.

Turn down so the water stays on a gentle simmer, and poach the chicken for 1 hour. Test for doneness by pulling away a leg from the body to check for pinkness inside the thigh.

Remove the chicken from the stock to a board and leave to cool. Meanwhile, turn up the heat under the pan of stock and allow it to bubble until it has reduced to 1 litre. Set it aside.

Remove the skin from the chicken and discard, and then pick all the flesh from the carcass. Cut it into small pieces.

To make the white sauce for the pie, melt the butter in a large saucepan. When it is sizzling, add the flour. Stir around until you have a thick paste. Add the mustard and combine. Gradually pour in the reserved chicken stock, beating it into the paste with a wooden spoon. Allow to cook, stirring, until the sauce has thickened sufficiently.

Chop the white part of the leeks into thin rounds. Melt a small knob of butter in a frying pan and fry the leeks over a medium heat until they are softened but be careful not to let them catch or brown. Tip them into the sauce and mix. Season with salt and black pepper.

Sprinkle flour over the work surface and roll out the pastry with a rolling pin. Place one pie dish upside down on the pastry to use as a template and cut 1cm wider than the dish around it.

Preheat the oven to 180°C/350°F/gas mark 4.

Divide the chicken evenly between the pie dishes, making sure there is an even mixture of white and brown meat. Pour over the creamy leek sauce.

Using a pastry brush, paint one side of each pastry circle with the beaten eggs.

Take a piece of the cut pastry and carefully lower over a pie dish, egg side down. Then, take a fork and crimp the edge of the pastry all around to ensure it sticks. Using a sharp knife, trim the edge so there is no overhang. Brush the top of the pie with more of the beaten egg.

Bake in the oven for around 20 minutes until the tops have risen and are golden.

STORECUPBOARD ESSENTIALS

I don't think there's a cook alive who doesn't have a list of essentials on standby for impromptu dinners. I always have the obvious things (flour, sugar, spaghetti, pesto, potatoes, Maldon sea salt) but there are a few others that can help you perform kitchen alchemy.

Pomegranate molasses to drizzle over halloumi and use in marinades and dressings.

Lemon juice in a bottle: better than a shrivelled and mouldy lemon in the fruit bowl.

Vegetable bouillon in powder form: I use it endlessly.

Chinese Shaoxing wine comes in a screw-top bottle, is best bought in Chinatown but is now in many supermarkets. Wonderful in stir-fries and good for risottos and sauces in place of sherry.

Tinned chickpeas are great to bulk out stews, add to curry sauces for last-minute vegetarian dishes, and whizz with olive oil for dips. Endless options, really.

Dijon mustard makes dressings and sauces taste so much better. Add a heaped tablespoon to lentils and goat's cheese for a quick salad.

Miso powder added to noodles or green vegetables gives you supper in five minutes.

TURKEY GRATIN

This is what we eat at my parents' house on Boxing Day. Always accompanied by a fluffy, butter-filled baked potato, this is a dish of leftover cooked turkey covered in a creamy, rich sauce made with stock and thickened with a roux. The top is strewn with grated cheese and over it all is a blanket of crisp, butter-fried breadcrumbs. It is an intensely comforting dish.

   Elizabeth David's version of the French classic *émincé de volaille* originally inspired this version, which is my mother's. There are two ways to make this: either with leftover meat or by poaching the turkey from scratch. If you do poach the turkey, you can then use the stock straight away in the sauce. (Of course this can be made with chicken, too.)

   I like to serve this with kale or spinach to counteract the richness.

SERVES 6–8 (IT IS VERY RICH)
**400g cooked turkey (if poaching
from scratch, you will need
1kg raw, bone-in pieces, such
as thighs)**
600ml stock of your choice
150ml whole milk
**65g butter, plus extra for
greasing**
75g plain flour
1 tbsp Dijon mustard
100g Cheddar, finely grated

For the topping
150g Cheddar, finely grated
**100g fried breadcrumbs (to
make your own, see method
below), or panko breadcrumbs**

SECRET
If you are making the
gratin in advance to serve
the next day, top up the
liquid to 1 litre in total for
the sauce, as it will thicken
considerably overnight.

METHOD
Preheat the oven to 180°C/350°F/gas mark 4.

Either chop the leftover meat and place in a buttered gratin dish, or poach 1kg turkey thighs by covering them with water and simmering for approximately 30 minutes until the meat is cooked. Reserve the cooking liquid for the sauce, tear the meat from the bones and place in the gratin dish, as above.

Mix together the stock and milk.

Meanwhile, melt the butter until it sizzles and sift in the flour – do sift, as it helps avoid lumps. Stir together rapidly, until a smooth paste is achieved. Then start to add the stock mixture. I like to start with about 150ml, just to get the sauce going. When that is mixed together, add about 250ml more and whisk this together, being sure to scrape the corners of the pan where the paste congregates. When it has started to thicken, add another big slosh of stock and vigorously whisk together.

Add the mustard and continue stirring until all the liquid has been added.

Add the cheese and beat into the sauce with a wooden spoon.

When the sauce is thick but still slightly runny, pour over the meat in the gratin dish and stir carefully together.

For the topping, strew the grated Cheddar over the gratin, then the fried breadcrumbs, and place in the oven for about 30 minutes, until the top is golden and bubbling. Do keep an eye on it, as it can burn in an instant.

TO MAKE YOUR OWN FRIED BREADCRUMBS
Either use prepared fresh breadcrumbs or make them yourself. Cut 250g white bread, remove the crusts and reduce to crumbs in the food processor, either with the blade or with the grating attachment: this will produce about 100g crumbs.

Place 50g butter in a frying pan and when melted, tip in the breadcrumbs and mix thoroughly. Keep an eye on them as they burn easily. They should take about 15 minutes to turn a dark golden colour.

COURGETTE AND PEA ORZOTTO

Orzotto isn't made with orzo – the tiny, Italian pasta – but with pearl barley ('orzo' is the Italian word for barley). Pearl barley is a grain that holds up a lot better to liquid than risotto rice. The pay-off is that you lose the unctuous creaminess of a risotto, but what you get in return is a lovely, resistant quality to the grain which, whilst still softened, holds its shape.

Orzotto has been a staple in my recipe head since I was a university student. It's cheap to buy and practically idiot-proof. That's because there's no great secret to producing a great orzotto. Unlike its kissing cousin, the risotto, it does not demand, or even need, dedicated wrist action or 45 minutes of close nurturing over the stove. You just add the hot liquid to the grains, mix it in and simmer away, pausing every so often when you pass the cooker to give it a stir and check it's not catching. It also cooks very quickly and you can be sitting down to eat in 30 minutes if you get a wiggle on.

SERVES 4
750ml vegetable or chicken
   stock
1 tbsp olive oil
1 onion, finely chopped
200g pearl barley
50ml white wine or pale sherry
   (Fino is delicious in this)
knob of butter
150g courgette, chopped into
   1cm slices, and then into
   cubes
150g frozen petits pois
50g Parmesan, grated
sea salt and freshly ground
   black pepper

METHOD
Heat the stock to a simmer.

Put a saucepan over a medium heat and add the olive oil. When it is heated, add the chopped onion and cook gently until it is translucent – about 10 minutes. (Don't let it brown, as this will colour the orzotto.)

When the onion has softened, add the barley grains and stir. Add the wine or sherry and let it reduce by half.

Then add all the hot stock and simmer away for about 20 minutes until the barley is soft but resistant.

Whilst the barley is cooking, fry the courgette cubes in the butter until soft but not browned. Defrost the peas by pouring boiling water over them in a metal bowl or pan, then drain.

When the barley is cooked, add the grated Parmesan and tip in the vegetables, reserving a few spoons of courgettes to pop on top as a garnish. Stir everything together and add salt and pepper to taste.

SQUASH STUFFED WITH CREAMY MUSHROOMS

Stuffed peppers were the bane of my life as a teenage vegetarian: practically raw pepper shells, filled with a claggy, inedible mixture of barely cooked rice, with bullet-hard peas and bits of pappy carrot, bound with egg. I swore I would never eat a stuffed vegetable as an adult.

I do love winter squash, though, and when I lived in New Jersey, there would be piles of squashes, gourds and pumpkins in all shades of orange, yellow, creams and green stacked up at roadside stands and in the pumpkin patches that proliferate along the highways.

So I thought a bit about what might go into that convenient hole that is left when all the seeds are scooped out, and decided that the answer might be mushrooms bound in a light cream sauce. I find this works wonderfully.

SERVES 4

2 small, round, striped squashes
1 tbsp olive oil
30g butter
250g mushrooms, chopped small
1 garlic clove, crushed and chopped
2 sprigs of thyme, leaves removed from the stems
sea salt and freshly ground black pepper
100ml single cream

METHOD

Preheat the oven to 180°C/350°F/gas mark 4.

Split each squash in half horizontally and scoop out the seeds. You will probably also need to level off the stem so that the top half can sit flat in the baking tray.

Brush each cut surface with oil and place the squash halves, cut-side up, in an ovenproof dish.

Set a frying pan over a medium heat and melt the butter until it fizzes. Tip in the mushrooms, garlic, thyme leaves and a good pinch of salt and some black pepper. Cook slowly until the mushrooms are soft, then add the cream and bring to a simmer. You want the cream to thicken slightly but not be runny. This should take about 5 minutes. The cream will thicken further on baking.

Scoop the mixture into the squash halves, cover tightly with foil and bake for about 1 hour, depending on the size.

VEGETARIAN RESTAURANTS IN SINGAPORE THAT DON'T MAKE YOU MISS MEAT

WHOLE EARTH PERANAKAN-THAI-VEGETARIAN RESTAURANT

This fusion of Thai and Straits Chinese food is something you will only find in Singapore. There are lots of braised beancurd and clever mushroom dishes, all bursting with flavour, and the emphasis is on clean food: no added MSG and no mock foods (no glutens, no fake chicken or fish).

76 Peck Seah Street, Singapore 079331; www.wholeearth.com.sg

GOKUL VEGETARIAN RESTAURANT, LITTLE INDIA

This may be a 21st-century take on an Indian restaurant, with Bouroullec-inspired plastic chairs, modern lampshades and waiters in snazzy uniforms, but, nonetheless, the food is immediately recognisable, with delicious dosas, an epic vegetarian version of chicken rice and very good murtabak.

19 Upper Dickson Road, Singapore 207478; www.gokulvegetarianrestaurant.com

LINGZHI

A very beige room and an unpromising location in an office block belies the extraordinary variety of food that appears on the menu here, with vegetables and mushrooms that will be new to a European palate. There is an emphasis on organic ingredients and I always, always overorder because everything sounds – and tastes – so good.

Liat Towers #05-01, 541 Orchard Road, Singapore 238881; www.lingzhivegetarian.com

MUSHROOMS ON TOAST, FOUR WAYS

For all the ways I know to cook mushrooms, there is something very pleasing about the simplicity of piling sautéed mushrooms onto a piece of perfect toast. I like, too, that not only can this be the ultimate indulgent supper for one, but also a delicious meal for friends gathered around the kitchen table. I particularly enjoy eating this in autumn, when mushrooms are in season. It's scrumptious, heart-warming and perfect for damp, foggy days.

I have lots of variations on this theme but the key to this dish is making sure that all your ingredients are as fresh and as good as possible. With simple food the flavours have really got to sing out, and skimping just makes the simplicity redundant.

Do choose good bread for this. Sourdough is excellent here, as is a close-crumbed rye or a grain-packed granary.

The method is similar in all cases: prepare white, chestnut and flat mushrooms by cutting them into thick slices and then slicing across to make cubes; tear oyster, trompettes de la mort or chanterelles into pieces. It's hard to be too generous when cooking mushrooms as they do cook down so much but, generally, I allow around 250g mushrooms per head.

Add a generous knob of butter and a tablespoon of olive oil to the pan and, when bubbling, tip in the mushrooms and cook gently until they are soft and give off their juices. Keep the heat on low-medium. You don't want the mushrooms to brown.

Season generously and tip onto toasted bread. A squeeze of lemon is always good at the end.

I've offered some variations here; all recipes serve four.

WITH PARSLEY AND GARLIC

1 garlic clove, crushed
very generous handful
**   flat-leaf parsley leaves, chopped**

METHOD
Add the garlic to the cooking mushrooms. Tip the mushrooms over the toast, and strew with the parsley.

WITH WHITE BEANS, KALE, CHEESE AND A BUTTERY SAUCE

400g tin cannellini beans
2 handfuls kale, shredded (central stem
   removed)
50g butter
50g hard cheese (Parmesan, Cheddar,
   Lancashire or ricotta salata are all good here)

METHOD

Add the beans, kale and 1 tbsp water to the
nearly-cooked mushrooms. Clamp a lid over the
pan for a few minutes until the kale is wilted.
Throw in the butter and allow it to melt. Taste and
season. Spoon the mixture over the toast, then
grate some cheese over the top.

WITH MADEIRA CREAM

1 shallot or small onion, finely chopped
2 garlic cloves, finely chopped
50ml Madeira, sherry or white wine
250ml single cream
fresh green herbs, if you have them
500g bag spinach leaves

METHOD

Before you add the mushrooms to the frying pan
sweat the shallot or onion and garlic in the butter
and olive oil over a medium heat until translucent.
Then tip in the mushrooms.

When they are softened, add the Madeira, sherry
or wine, turn the heat to high and bubble it down
for a few minutes to burn off the alcohol.

Turn the heat down to medium, add the cream and
stir around. Add the herbs, if using. Let bubble for
a few minutes while you rinse the spinach. Throw
the wet spinach in a pan with the lid on (no extra
water) and remove, once wilted (2–3 minutes), to
a colander. Press out any extra water.

Check the seasoning of the mushrooms. If your
sauce has bubbled down too much and is looking
gloopy, add a bit of hot water to thin it out.

Divide the spinach over the toast and heap over
the mushrooms and cream. Add a generous twist
of black pepper.

BAKED CHICKEN THIGHS, THREE WAYS

I think we all have evenings where we optimistically invite friends round for supper and then get stuck in the office, or on the phone, or on a bus that doesn't seem to move. Bolting into a supermarket an hour before my guests are due to arrive, because I have no time to prepare my planned meal, often results in my standing there like a rabbit in headlights, wondering if cheese is ever an acceptable supper option (well, yes; but also, no).

In this situation I often cook chicken thighs. They are one of those seemingly boring cuts of meat that undergo a magical transformation when shoved in a hot oven with aromatic herbs and lots of butter and oil. The darker meat is juicy, full of flavour, and the skin crisps up beautifully. There are also lots of bones to gnaw: I always think getting down and dirty with your food is the sign of a good kitchen supper amongst friends.

I always allow two thighs per person, and then several over. (So much nicer to be able to offer seconds, rather than attempting portion control.) Before cooking them, I usually turn them over and use scissors to trim off some of the skin that is tucked under, to allow the meat to cook evenly on the bottom.

Couscous, bulgur wheat or quinoa goes very well with chicken.

> **SECRET**
> Please do buy free-range chicken: not only it is a Good Thing to do, those legs work a lot harder and consequently the meat tastes much better.

BASIC RECIPE

SERVES 4

10 chicken thighs
**50g softened butter (zap in
  microwave for 20 seconds
  if necessary)**
2 tbsp olive oil
**sea salt and freshly ground
  black pepper**

METHOD

Preheat the oven to 180°C/350°F/gas mark 4.

Place the chicken thighs in a roasting tin or dish. Rub the butter
into the thighs and drizzle with the oil. Liberally salt and pepper
the chicken.

Bake for 45 minutes, or until cooked through.

WITH GNOCCHI, LEMON AND ROSEMARY

4–5 sprigs of rosemary
**1 packet vacuum-packed
  gnocchi**
**grated zest and juice from
  ½ lemon**

METHOD

Follow the basic recipe, adding
the rosemary to the baking dish
with the chicken.

Whilst the chicken is cooking,
poach the gnocchi according to
packet instructions.

When the chicken is done,
remove to a plate to rest.
Increase the oven temperature
to 200°C/400°F/gas mark 6 and
add the gnocchi to the juices
in the chicken dish. Bake for
10 minutes, or until the gnocchi
is browned.

Remove the dish from the oven
and return the chicken to it. Add
the lemon zest and juice. Serve at
the table.

WITH PASTA AND GREEN HERBS

**400g dried pasta: penne or
macaroni**

**2 generous handfuls mixed
  chopped, soft green herbs,
  e.g. chervil, tarragon, thyme,
  parsley**

METHOD

Cook the chicken following the
basic recipe. Fifteen minutes
from the end of the cooking time,
cook the pasta according to the
packet instructions and drain,
reserving a cup of the cooking
water for later.

When the chicken is done,
scatter over the herbs and serve
with the pasta. Add the reserved
pasta water to the baking dish,
scraping up all the good bits
from the bottom, and spoon the
juices over the chicken.

WITH OLIVES, LEMON AND OREGANO

**generous handful fresh
  oregano, leaves finely chopped**
5 lemons
**1 cup mixed green and black
  olives, pitted**
1 tbsp chopped flat-leaf parsley

METHOD

Reserve 1 tbsp oregano, then mix
the rest with the softened butter
and apply to the chicken thighs,
following the basic recipe.

Quarter 4 of the lemons and add
to the chicken dish before it goes
in the oven.

Zest the final lemon.

Fifteen minutes before the
chicken comes out, add the
olives to the baking dish.

When the dish is finally removed,
scatter over the lemon zest,
parsley and remaining oregano.

SLOW-COOKED TOMATO SAUCE

This sauce is one of my bedrock recipes. It's delicious on its own but it also forms the base of so much that I like to cook – and eat. Once a month or so I cook up a huge vat of the stuff, freezing it into two-person portions, so there is always something to eat in the house without resorting to takeaway menus or ready meals. (Don't be tempted to freeze large containers-full, even if you are a big family – they take forever to defrost. It's much better to freeze in small portions.)

I was taught to make this by my mother, and I've been cooking vats of it since I was in my early teens. The ingredients are things I think most of us would be able to find in the most basic of storecupboards.

The most important thing about this sauce is that you should cook it for at least 1 hour and add a little sugar to counteract the metallic taste of the tinned tomatoes. I just do not understand the countless recipes out there that call for tinned tomatoes and then require only 20 minutes' cooking time. All that can possibly give is a raw, harsh flavour. I like quite a lot of onion in my sauce, both for depth of flavour and for texture – it makes the sauce thicker.

SERVE 4 AS A PASTA SAUCE
slosh of olive oil
1 large onion, chopped
2 garlic cloves, crushed
  (optional)
3 x 400g tins tomatoes
  (my optimal combination
  is 1 tin of whole tomatoes,
  1 of chopped tomatoes and
  1 of cherry tomatoes)
passata (optional)
large squeeze of tomato purée
1 tsp sugar
sea salt and freshly ground
  black pepper

SECRET
Don't worry about using expensive branded tinned tomatoes, or any other hand-plucked-by-organic-virgins-in-Italy ones, either. Whatever is cheap on the shelf at the supermarket will do fine.

METHOD
Put a nice big saucepan (I prefer wider to higher, as it cooks down more quickly) over a medium-high heat and add a generous slosh of basic olive oil.

When it's hot, tip in the onion, turn the heat right down, and sweat (i.e. slow-cook in oil) until translucent, pushing it around from time to time. This takes at least 20 minutes. Cook the onion too hot and fast and it will brown and caramelise. You want the onion to be soft and colourless. (You want it nice and soft because once it hits the tomatoes it won't get any softer.) Add the garlic, if using, 5 minutes before the onion is done.

Then pour in the tomatoes, add a big slug of passata (if you have it), the tomato purée and sugar. Get it to simmering point (slow bubbling), then turn the heat to low-medium and leave to simmer away, uncovered.

Do keep stirring regularly as the sauce has a nasty habit of catching; turn down the heat if you think it is boiling too fast. I also use a splatter guard, as it bubbles away like a tub of volcanic gloop and you will end up with tomato-sauce splodges everywhere, otherwise. After about 20 minutes, break up any whole tomatoes with the back of a spoon and continue to cook.

After about 45 minutes, add salt and black pepper, to taste. Check the seasoning and add a wee bit more sugar if you think it needs it. Allow it to cook for a little longer – I reckon it takes a total of 1 hour to reduce properly and become sweet, thick and unctuous.

SECRETS

You could also add a glass of red wine to the onions once they are cooked, reducing it by half before adding the tomatoes. I sometimes add whole, dried chillies to the softening onion mixture. Once, I had run out of sugar, so I added a splodge of ketchup. Another time, I used Sriracha chilli sauce instead, which worked brilliantly.

Other than eating this plain with pasta, I've liquidised it to make tomato soup; shoved it through a sieve for a more refined sauce; added cream for a pretty, pink, pasta sauce; used it as the base for lasagne (see page 70); made a Moroccan-inspired sauce by changing the spicing; used it as a base for curries; made enchiladas with it; baked it in nachos; poured it over baked potatoes ... it's the sauce that just keep on giving.

PRESENTS FOR GODCHILDREN

When I was little, parcels arriving in the post, addressed to me and covered in stamps, always promised something wonderful. I decided that when I had godchildren of my own I would be a prolific sender of brown-paper-wrapped parcels. Travelling around the world as I do, I pick up gifts from all manner of places and wing them, tied up with string and good wishes, back to my five godchildren in England. In particular I pick up clothes from other cultures to fire their imaginations. Here are some of my all-star gifts.

SINGAPORE In the heart of Little India is Mustafa Centre. It truly is a department store, in that amongst its chaotic aisles and almost impenetrable layout one can buy mangoes and electronics, lipsticks and gold jewellery. (There's a brilliant kitchen equipment department, too.) And somewhere deep in the heart of the piles of children's clothes are racks of lovely, embroidered salwar kameez, most for less than £15.

145 Syed Alwi Road, Singapore 207704; www.mustafa.com.sg

For satin cheongsams, fans and those pretty folding paper parasols that I coveted as a child, I head to Chinatown to the tourist-bait stalls of Pagoda Street.

Chinatown MRT

MOROCCO Whilst some derive great pleasure from navigating the narrow lanes of the souks in Marrakesh to haggle endlessly, I've discovered that I prefer the quieter pleasure of shopping in the Ensemble Artisanal where there is a fixed-price shop selling only Moroccan, embroidered leather slippers in the brightest jewel tones.

Rue de la Kasbah, Marrakesh, Morocco

BARCELONA I lived in espadrilles during the summer as a child, and so I always pick up some godchild-friendly, handmade pairs with pretty, tape-ribbon ties from La Manual Alpargatera in the Barri Gòtic. Founded after the Civil War, it is Barcelona's most iconic espadrille store.

Carrer Avinyó 7, 08002 Barcelona; www.lamanualalpargatera.es

BALI The Carga Lifestyle Store in Seminyak looks like a beautiful Balinese home, hung with red lanterns. Inside are all sorts of treasure from rose-quartz earrings, to wooden platters made from local wood. It's here I bought a lovely handmade doll for Clementine, made by and for a street-kids project. It also stocks silk, batik romper suits by local childrenswear label Coco & Ginger; hand-embroidered party dresses and frilled knickers for infants.

Jalan Petitenget, 886, Kerobokan; www.cargabali.com

NEW YORK If you have children who are obsessed with the NYPD and the NYFD, then the NYC Firestore is the place to come: they sell anything and everything related to New York's Finest and New York's Bravest. I've found that die-cast fire engines and logo T-shirts go down particularly well and I am particularly fond of the NYFD toddler T-shirts that say 'Stay Back 200 Feet' on the reverse. My feelings exactly, when presented with a chocolate-covered urchin.

17 Greenwich Avenue, New York, NY 10014; www.nyfirestore.com

NEW POTATO, GOAT'S CHEESE AND THYME TART

This is the simplest of simple recipes, yet the deliciousness of its transformation – from inedible, raw ingredients to soft, melting, crispy, unctuous, salty moreishness – is something close to alchemy.

I'm afraid it does require a mandoline or a food processor with a slicing attachment unless you possess infinite patience, a very sharp knife and a true eye for slicing potatoes super thin.

SERVES 4–6

1 small bag new potatoes (approx. 500g)
½ slab ready-made puff pastry (approx. 250g)
butter, for greasing
flour, for dusting
1 goat's cheese (the kind in a log with a rind, not the spreadable stuff), thinly sliced
several sprigs of thyme
splash of olive oil
sea salt and freshly ground black pepper
1 egg

METHOD

Preheat the oven to 180°C/350°F/gas mark 4.

Slice the potatoes. I recommend using either the slicing attachment on a food processor or, like me, risking your fingertips and using a mandoline. It's the work of a few minutes to slice a small bag of new potatoes into uniform pieces. The key word there is uniform: you need the slices to be the same thickness so that they cook through evenly. About the width of a two-pence piece.

Grease a baking tray with butter. If you plan to serve this tart on a platter rather than the baking tray, place a piece of greaseproof paper or baking parchment on the tray so that you can easily transfer it.

Take the puff pastry and roll it on a floured board until thin but still small enough to fit on the baking tray. Transfer the pastry over to the greased baking tray, then lightly score a box about 2.5cm inside the edges. Layer the potato slices onto the pastry within the scored box and arrange the goat's cheese slices on top.

Strew over the sprigs of thyme, splash on some olive oil, and liberally add salt and black pepper.

Beat the egg with a fork and brush over the pastry border.

Bake for about 15–20 minutes.

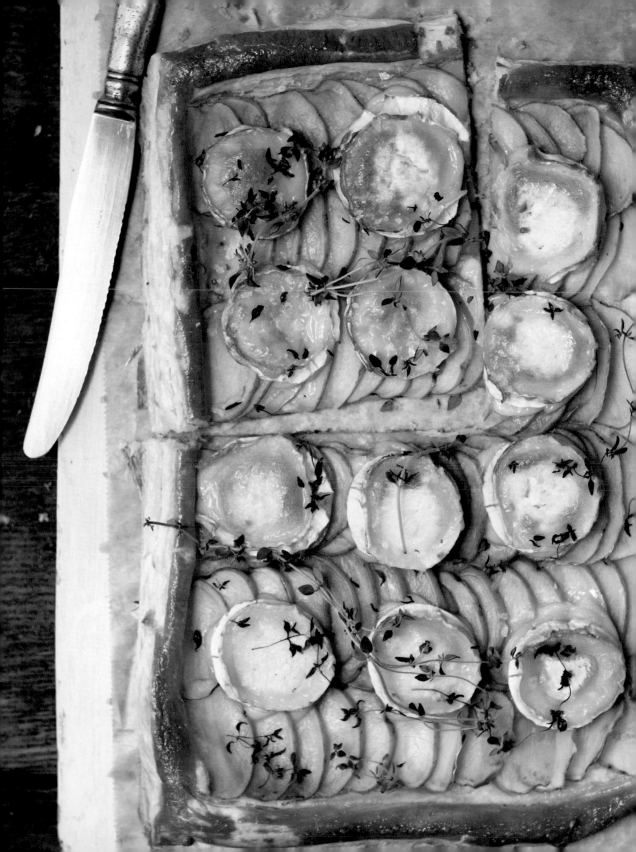

WEEKEND ENTERTAINING

A lovely, long lunch with a big group of people is one of my favourite ways to entertain family and friends at weekends. It's comforting, familiar and relaxed, often going on all afternoon, as we lean back, kick off our shoes under the table (avoiding the children and dogs inevitably hiding there) and get stuck into delicious food.

Sunday lunch, in particular, can be daunting to plan and prepare but, with a few tricks and some planning ahead it's often one of the simplest meals to assemble.

I've been asked to weekend lunches where there has been a starter, five vegetables to go with the main course, umpteen sauces and accompaniments,

followed by a tricky dessert and a selection of cheese and bread that I could live off for a week. I say, life is waaay too short. I'd rather be talking to my friends than hovering, puce and sweating, over the stove. Ditch the starter, make loads of potatoes, choose two vegetables at the most and forget any fancy-pants sauces.

In the winter, make a one dish dessert, like my Eve's Pudding (see page 140), that can be prepared in advance and popped in the oven when the main course is served. In the summer, fruit salad, good ice cream, or a bowl of berries are all perfectly acceptable desserts. Or, make like the French and buy a tart from a pâtisserie.

If you like to serve cheese instead of (or as well as) pudding, choose just one piece of something delicious. Buy an oozy slab of Brie at least two days in advance, or a chunk of farmhouse Cheddar and serve with grapes, chutney or membrillo – the Spanish quince paste – and the bread you bought to go with the main course.

If only one or two people amongst you are vegetarian, please don't worry about providing an extra dish for them: in all my years as a veggie, I was more than happy to eat a plate of delicious Sunday veg. If you *would* like to make something for the vegetarian contingent, make a cauliflower cheese with lots of sauce, or a gratin with

eggs and cream as one of your vegetable sides, then everyone is happy.

On the subject of the night before, try to lay the table then, if you can. I often peel the potatoes then, too (in front of the television) and leave them soaking in cold water overnight. Don't prep any other vegetables in advance: soaking leaches out vitamins and they can go flabby.

I always have a friend who insists on bringing something with them and won't take no for an answer, so I suggest they either buy the cheese, something for pud, or some excellent bread.

Above all, try to relax: it's the weekend, after all ...

LAMB CUTLETS ON MASHED BUTTER BEANS

In this dish I particularly like the contrast between the melting, tender meat and the silky-but-rough mashed beans. (It's important to season the meat and the beans properly to really bring out the contrasts.)

Hot or cold, cutlets are always delicious. When I cooked the cutlets for the photo opposite, I had some left over. The next morning I discovered four gnawed bones neatly lined up in the dish: my best friend had decided that they were the perfect post-party midnight snack.

SERVES 4

a little olive oil, for cooking
8 lamb cutlets
sea salt and freshly ground black pepper
a few snipped chives, to garnish

For the butter beans
2 x 400g tins butter beans, rinsed and drained
2 tbsp grassy olive oil

METHOD

Put a heavy pan over a high heat – I use a cast-iron griddle.

Massage a little olive oil into the cutlets, then put them into the hot pan, in batches. Sprinkle over some salt and a generous grind of black pepper. Cook for 3–4 minutes on each side (season each side) for lovely pink middles, and around 5 for well-done meat. Try not to move them around or they won't crisp up properly.

Meanwhile, tip all the beans into a large bowl with the olive oil and some salt and pepper and squash roughly with a fork until they are about half-mashed.

Grab a large platter and turn out the mashed beans onto it. Place the cooked lamb cutlets on top of the beans, tip over any cooking juices and sprinkle over the chives.

> ### SECRET
> A recipe that looks impressive, tastes delicious and only takes 20 minutes to make is one that everyone should have up their sleeve. And this is one such gem.

ROAST LAMB WITH ANCHOVIES, ROSEMARY AND GARLIC

I have always cooked roast lamb studded with slivers of garlic and massaged with a paste of mashed anchovies and butter. I promise there will be no fishy reek when you taste this – just deliciousness. (I believe the method is Gascon in origin.) All you need to make a success of this is a small, very sharp paring knife to make slits in the skin into which you insert the garlic slivers. (Use a knife that is too big and your garlic will get lost in the cuts.)

   A pestle and mortar is helpful for bashing together the butter and anchovies, but it's certainly not essential.

SERVES 6–8 COMFORTABLY

6 garlic cloves, peeled
several sprigs of rosemary
1 leg of lamb, approx. 2kg
100g butter, softened
1 x 50g tin of anchovies in
   olive oil, drained

METHOD

Preheat the oven to 180°C/350°F/gas mark 4.

The cooking time for roast lamb is around 20–25 minutes per 500g, plus another 20 minutes on top. So allow about 1 hour 35 minutes if you like your lamb nicely pink. If you are more of a well-done person, then add on another 20 minutes.

Slice the garlic into slivers. Pull off little sprigs of rosemary from their stems.

Make a series of incisions in the lamb about 2.5cm long all over the surface, about 5cm apart, and stick the garlic into these, along with sprigs of rosemary.

Mash together the butter and anchovies into a paste and spread this all over the surface of the meat.

Place in the oven and cook according to the instructions above. Don't forget to factor in another 20 minutes to allow the meat to relax and release its juices, once it has come out of the oven. This will also make it easier to carve.

SECRET

The anchovies are the magic ingredient here. Somehow they become far, far more than the sum of their parts, melting away to an umami-rich note and lifting the flavour of the lamb.

FLEA MARKETS FOR PICKING UP VINTAGE CHINA, GLASS, JEWELLERY AND CLOTHES

USA

MELROSE TRADING POST, LOS ANGELES

The Sunday flea market each week at Melrose and North Fairfax in West Hollywood is as notable for the celebs you can spot trying on vintage cowboy boots and the like, as it is for the actual stalls. It's probably the most expensive flea market I've ever visited but, if you rummage, there are some bargains to be had, especially in homewares.

7850 Melrose Avenue, Los Angeles, CA 90046; open Sunday 9am to 5pm; www.melrosetradingpost.org

PASADENA ROSE BOWL VINTAGE FAIR, LOS ANGELES

My absolute favourite place for vintage and second-hand bargains in LA is the Pasadena Rose Bowl Vintage Fair, which has more than 2,500 stalls. Whether you are searching for vintage Harley Davidson parts or a pretty fifties dress, this is a second-hand goldmine.

Rose Bowl Stadium, 1001 Rose Bowl Drive, Pasadena, CA 91103; open on the second Sunday of each month, 9am to 4.30pm; www.rgcshows.com/rosebowl.aspx

THE ANTIQUES GARAGE, HELL'S KITCHEN FLEA MARKET, NEW YORK

When I lived in New York, I would pop in to The Antiques Garage every weekend to browse the 100-plus vendors. The breadth of items on offer suits my magpie mind perfectly: there are fine silver items, eclectic antiques, furniture, rugs and prints; plus vintage jewellery, handbags, fabrics and clothes.

12 West 25th Street (between 6th and 7th Avenues); open Saturday and Sunday, 9am to 5pm; www.hellskitchenfleamarket.com

BROOKLYN FLEA, NEW YORK

I went to the very first Brooklyn Flea in Fort Greene, and bought vintage jewellery and kitchen bowls. It's now expanded to DUMBO (Down Under Manhattan Bridge Overpass), where you'll find the best stuff for your home. Great food trucks too.

Empire-Fulton Ferry State Park, DUMBO; open Sunday 11am to 6pm; www.brooklynflea.com

BANGKOK

CHATUCHAK WEEKEND MARKETA

One of the largest markets in the world, this has an entire interior-design section, as well as an antiques one. Buy a map on arrival and wear flat shoes. I've bought kitchen equipment and wonderful things for my house here.

Next to Kamphaenpech station (MRT); open Saturday and Sunday, 6am to 6pm; www.chatuchak.org

UK

LEWES FLEA MARKET, LEWES

Open every day, this is a wonderful place to pick up curiosities and second-hand furniture for the home, as well as, occasionally, vintage fashion and jewellery. I've bought old scent bottles (to use as flower vases) and wonderful vintage china here for bargain prices.

14a Market Street, Lewes, East Sussex BN7 2NB; open daily 10am to 5pm; www.flea-markets.co.uk

INDOOR FLEA MARKET AT ASHTON GATE STADIUM, BRISTOL

A once-a-month flea market, which attracts both private sellers and dealers from all over the south-west of England, it is particularly good for vintage garden furniture and china, but there is lots of great vintage clothing and jewellery, too.

Ashton Gate Stadium, Ashton, Bristol BS3 2EJ; open one Saturday a month, 9am to 3.30pm; www.bristolfleamarket.co.uk

FOOLPROOF ROAST CHICKEN

A good roast chicken recipe is an excellent thing to have in reserve. Wherever you may find yourself cooking, it's unlikely that you won't have an oven and a dish that can go inside it. And that's all you need to roast a chicken.

Like so much of my kitchen lore, I learnt my roast chicken method from my mother, and it has never failed me. In fact, it's less of a recipe and more of a kitchen mantra.

It is simply this: allow 20 minutes in the oven per pound (or half kilo), add an extra 20 on top, and remember that the cooking time should finish about 20 minutes before you wish to eat it, to let the meat (which tightens during cooking) relax, allowing the juices to flow for your gravy.

Once you have that committed to memory, you will always be able to roast a chicken. Of course there are other things that help: I like to massage 100g butter all over the skin of the chicken, thighs and legs, as well as the breasts; stuff both halves of a lemon inside, and strew some rosemary or tarragon branches around the dish. A liberal application of crunchy sea salt all over the buttered bird is essential, and a few grinds of black pepper would not go astray.

And that is it: no great secret, no complicated process. But it will give you an incredibly moist chicken; delectable, crisp skin and lots of buttery, lemony pan juices for the gravy. And the gratitude of your hungry friends and family.

MUSHROOM GRAVY

This intensely savoury gravy is perfect for any vegetarian or vegan who may be sitting around your Sunday lunch table: I've found that most vegetarians would infinitely prefer a plate of delicious Sunday vegetables for lunch as opposed to an entirely different main course. The gravy is the key part of this theory: a dish of vegetables and roast potatoes inevitably needs some sauce and, of course, most gravies contain meat stock and the scrapings from the meat pan. So I've come up with this 100-per-cent no-meat gravy, which is a hell of a lot easier than having to knock up a separate main course. Oh, and it freezes like a dream.

MAKES ENOUGH FOR AT LEAST 6 PEOPLE
500g mushrooms (I like mixed white and flat)
2 tbsp vegetable oil
sea salt and freshly ground black pepper
500ml vegetable stock
1 tbsp dark soy sauce
2 tbsp cornflour
4 tbsp hot water

METHOD
Very finely mince the mushrooms (this is best done in a food processor), reserving a handful of whole white mushrooms.

In a large frying pan, heat the oil and add the minced mushrooms with a good pinch of salt. Turn the heat down and slowly cook the mushrooms. The key here is to sweat the juices from them without too much evaporation.

Heat the stock and soy sauce in a large saucepan and, when the mushrooms are softened, tip them and their cooking juices into the stock pan with the soy sauce and leave to simmer. Roughly chop the remaining mushrooms into small pieces, add to the pan and cook for another 5 minutes.

Sift (this is very important) the cornflour into a small bowl and add the hot water, stirring briskly. When mixed, pour into the large saucepan and stir until the sauce thickens. Taste and season with salt and black pepper.

ROAST HAND AND SPRING OF PORK

When thinking about a Sunday joint of meat for a lunch party, it's always tempting to go for beef – maybe a sirloin or rib – or a leg of lamb, but the former can be wallet-tighteningly expensive, and the latter too small for a large group, and both need precise timings to ensure the meat is cooked the way you like, pink or otherwise.

I like to serve roast pork (although do check with your guests first, as it's the meat that comes with the most dietary issues) because it needs lots of cooking – pink pork is an absolute no-no – which means no complicated timings. It also makes delicious, rich gravy and, of course, gives you a pile of fabulous crackling to chew on.

Most people buy a leg of pork to roast, but I prefer the lesser-known, and much cheaper 'hand and spring', a cut from the front leg of the pig, just below the shoulder. In America it is known as Boston butt – not because it is from the rump but because once upon a time this cut was stored in barrels.

You can cook it one of two ways: either very long and slow at about 120°C/250°F/ gas mark ½, so it falls almost in shreds (it's no coincidence that Boston butt is used for barbecue in the Deep South), and that's the way most British cookbooks will suggest; or, you can roast it as you would any normal joint.

I prefer the latter, as it seems more Sunday-ish. You'll need to order it from your butcher – this is not a cut that you will find in the supermarket chiller. He will ask you if you want it on the bone, or off and rolled.

I like getting it on the bone, as it is guaranteed to cook all the way through – the bone acts as a conductor for heat, you get lots more crackling and I like the generous look of a big joint of meat. Boned and rolled is neater, though, and much easier to carve, as you will get perfect slices.

Either way, tell the butcher how many people you are feeding and he will suggest a suitable piece of meat. (A hand and spring should be able to feed six to twelve people.) Do make sure you ask the butcher to score the skin for crackling. I've forgotten in the past and, take it from me, it's not a simple task getting to grips with a Stanley knife and a piece of pig.

To ensure lovely, crispy crackling, you need to rub a little oil into the skin, and then rub in lots of flaked sea salt – I always use Maldon salt.

When you pick up your joint from the butcher, ask the exact weight. (It's quite tricky to balance a large joint on a set of domestic scales.) You need to allow 25 minutes per 500g, with an extra 25 minutes on top, and at least 30 minutes to rest out of the oven before you serve it. This allows the meat to relax, making it juicier and easier to carve. I would count on at least four hours in total, and probably five.

To cook it, preheat the oven to 200°C/400°F/ gas mark 6 and cook the joint for 25 minutes on this high heat to get the crackling off to a good start. Then turn the oven down to 180°C/350°F/ gas mark 4 for the rest of the cooking time.

I like to carve the meat away from the table. If it is on the bone, I remove the crackling first – you'll find that it lifts off quite easily when a knife slides underneath. Then simply cut the meat into chunks, and use kitchen scissors to cut up the crackling. I pile everything onto a platter, so that everyone can help themselves at the table, family-style.

Roast pork is traditionally served with apple sauce (see opposite). Roast or Hedgehog Potatoes (see pages 100 and 101), cauliflower cheese, and peas or green beans are delicious accompaniments.

APPLE SAUCE

This is one of the most versatile sauces and, once you have it under your cooking belt, you can knock it up without a recipe in a matter of minutes for both savoury and sweet purposes. I serve it with roast pork and roast goose; it's wonderful spooned over yogurt in the mornings, and I use it in my Blackberry and Apple Trifle (see page 126). It also freezes well, but do remember to label it, as frozen apple sauce looks like it could be chicken stock. How many this serves will depend on what you're using it for, but this quantity would be enough for six at Sunday lunch.

SERVES 6

2 large Bramley cooking apples (about 500g)
20ml water
1 tsp sugar, or to taste
squeeze of lemon juice

METHOD

Core and peel the apples and cut into small chunks. Tip into a small saucepan with the water, sugar and the lemon juice and simmer over a medium heat. You can either cook it down to a purée, or leave it with some pieces still whole.

Do taste the sauce and adjust the sweetness according to your taste: I like mine quite sharp, so you may need to add more sugar if you have a sweet tooth.

CAULIFLOWER PUREE

After years in the culinary wilderness, cauliflower is now recognised as a nutritional wonderfood, lauded for its filling but low carb-ness and packed with fibre, vitamin C and potential cancer-busting properties. In this recipe I promptly lower some of that nutritional appeal by loading it with cream and butter. I do like a little indulgence alongside my vitamins.

I cook this at every opportunity: it's wonderful with pretty much every roast meat, makes a perfect, fluffier replacement for mashed potato alongside a stew, and is delicious paired with mushrooms, in any guise. (You'll need a food processor or mouli-légumes. A stick or goblet blender is disastrous as it just chops rather than purées the cauliflower.)

It also makes a lovely soup if you thin it down with vegetable stock and a little whole milk at the end.

SERVES 4–6 AS A SIDE DISH
1 medium cauliflower, approx. 750g
50g butter, plus a little extra to serve
2 tbsp double cream
sea salt and white pepper (not essential, but more aesthetically pleasing than black)

METHOD
Take the cauliflower, cut out the core and divide into florets. Place in a saucepan and add about 8cm water. Simmer away with the lid on until the cauliflower is completely soft. You do not want any hint of al dente here. Drain the cauliflower over a bowl to catch the cooking water, which you want to keep.

Prepare your food processor or mouli-légumes (hand mill). Add the cauliflower, butter and the double cream to the mixer bowl. Whizz it all up. If it seems too thick, add a small ladle of the reserved cooking water. Add salt and whizz again. Check the seasoning, adding more if necessary.

Serve with a knob of butter on top. Snipped chives look pretty, too.

This can be made in advance and reheated, as I often do, to no ill effect, in the microwave.

SHREDDED, SAUTEED BRUSSELS SPROUTS WITH ALMONDS

I loathe and abhor Brussels sprouts. They resemble nothing so much as boiled budgerigar heads and their sulphurous reek is a Proustian return to the school dining room.

Or I thought so until I ate a plate of Brussels, finely sliced and stir-fried in rapeseed oil. What a revelation! Gone was the pappy texture and bitter taste and, in their place, were fresh, al dente greens with just an elusive hint of that brassica bitterness.

You'll need either a mandoline, or a very sharp knife and almost infinite patience.

SERVES 6 AS A SIDE DISH
300g Brussels sprouts
2 tbsp rapeseed or olive oil
30g flaked almonds
squeeze of lemon juice
sea salt and freshly ground black pepper

METHOD
The secret is to slice the sprouts as finely as possible: I use a mandoline to get them almost paper thin. Then simply add the rapeseed or olive oil to a large frying pan or wok, heat it until it smokes and tumble in your sliced Brussels sprouts. Don't push them around too much: you want some to catch, so you get a delicious frizzled, browned crispness to the edges. They take 15–20 minutes.

Just before you think they are done, tip in the almonds. A squeeze of lemon juice, a little salt and black pepper and they are ready.

PERFECT ROAST POTATOES

There are many recipes claiming to produce the perfect roast potato, but it really isn't complicated. There is no special ingredient that guarantees results: I don't call for goose fat, or polenta, or dustings of flour – just potatoes and hot oil. Olive oil, if you like. Rosemary sprigs in the oil if you fancy it.

The secret to a really crispy outside and melting middle is simple: cook them properly. There is no way you can get perfect roast potatoes in under an hour.

Don't be parsimonious. I allow at least six pieces of potato a head, and usually more. Bank on about 1.5–2kg potatoes for six people. (You'll need the biggest roasting tin you can get in your oven.) Cut them into chunks and parboil them almost to the point of being cooked through. If you forget about the potatoes and overcook them, it doesn't matter; just be careful not to break the pieces up as you drain them.

The single most important part of cooking roast potatoes is to ensure that you slide them into very hot oil. So, preheat the oven to 180°C/350°F/gas mark 4, cover the bottom of the roasting tin with 0.5cm oil and heat for 5–10 minutes until it sizzles.

Then carefully add the potatoes. Do add any broken pieces, as these will be your crispy bits. Be careful, as the oil will spit dreadfully. Turn them over and around so each potato is covered in hot oil. Roast for about 20 minutes, then turn them over. Turn them again at 40. Check them at 1 hour: they may be ready.

When they are perfectly crispy, tip them out into a serving dish and sprinkle some sea salt over them.

MASHED PEAS

This is not a recipe so much as a serving suggestion, but it is one that lifts the peas from mundane accompaniment to a delicious dish in its own right.

All you need to do is cook the peas, as normal (and I just use garden peas here, not petits pois as I would if serving them straight), tip them into a food processor with the leaves from a sprig or two of mint and pulse two or three times. This chops up the peas but doesn't purée them completely.

Tip them out into a serving dish, add some salt and black pepper and a little knob of butter. Garnish with some sprigs of mint.

SECRET

No one ever complained about discovering a roast potato in the kitchen a few hours after lunch, so err on the side of generosity and make plenty. Besides, Sunday lunch is all about making people content and no one was ever made happy by watching their host dole out three potatoes to each guest and then remove an empty serving plate to the kitchen.

HEDGEHOG POTATOES
(OR HASSELBACK, IF YOU MUST)

Okay, purists call these Hasselback potatoes. But I think hedgehog is much more fun. And far more appealing, especially if feeding children or fussy eaters. It's all in the sell, after all. You get a lot of crispiness, which contrasts with the lovely, soft inside: far more crunch, in fact, than a classic roast spud.

There are various ways of making these, and I am sure that the Swedish restaurant that claims them as their invention (Hasselbacken, in Stockholm) would not be altogether happy with my version. But no matter, they pleaseth me and mine, and that is all there is to it. Plus, as a special bonus, my version cooks very quickly, as well as being extraordinarily delicious. Go on, you know you want to ...

It is a recipe of simplicity, so I am not going to mess around here. I usually allow at least 200g per head. I also find that this recipe works equally well with both old and new potatoes.

potatoes (any kind but not too small; around 200g per head)
oil, for roasting (I prefer olive but vegetable works just as well)
sea salt

METHOD
Preheat the oven to 180°C/350°F/gas mark 4.

Take a very sharp knife and a rounded wooden spoon. Use the sharp knife to halve the potatoes lengthways (if their shape allows), then place a half, cut-side-down, in the bowl of the spoon. Cut lots of thin, parallel, almost-slices through the rounded side. The cuts should be almost, but not quite, to the bottom. Be careful not to go all the way.

When you are half-way through prepping the potatoes, pour lots of olive oil into a high-sided metal baking tray, and pop in the hot oven. (The oil needs to be at least 0.5cm deep.)

When all your potatoes have been pre-hedgehogged, take out your now-very-hot, oil-filled baking tray and carefully add the potatoes, cut-side-up. I do not recommend tipping the potatoes all at once into the oil. Hot oil spits. Tongs are helpful here, if you have them.

Once in the tray, wiggle the potatoes about with a spoon or tongs so they are covered in the lovely, hot oil and then bake for about 45 minutes. Check on them after about 25 and give the tray a good shake to stop the bottoms sticking. Overcooking is better than undercooking.

Once they have been taken out of the oven, sprinkle with lots of sea salt.

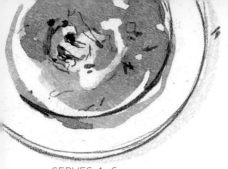

MUSHROOM SOUP FOR MUSHROOM-OPHOBES

If asked to come up with the menu for my final meal, this soup would be a strong contender for the first course. It's intensely, luxuriously mushroom-y, and is a pleasingly proper, mushroom-grey colour with little black flecks from the mushroom gills. When left overnight, it thickens considerably and makes a rather good sauce for chicken.

The recipe below is adapted from one of my all-time favourite cookbooks: Jane Grigson's *The Mushroom Feast*, which I bought in my first year at university, naughtily using the book bursary I was awarded for my theology degree. (Grigson actually found it first in Elizabeth David's *French Provincial Cooking*.)

What separates it from other mushroom soups is its secret ingredient: a thick slice of bread. The most extraordinary thing is that there is no trace whatsoever of the taste or texture of the bread upon eating.

I've had great success in cooking this soup for avowed mushroom avoiders. And so I'd like to dedicate this recipe to the memory of our friend, Sean Donovan, who was killed in an accident in the summer of our second year at university. He hated mushrooms but loved this soup.

SERVES 4–6

50g butter
350g mushrooms, chopped
(I like mixed large, flat, white mushrooms and chestnut, to get the best flavour)
2 tbsp chopped flat-leaf parsley leaves (plus extra, to serve, if you like)
1 small garlic clove, chopped
scraping of nutmeg
1 litre good stock (I'm afraid Jane would turn in her grave, as I use bouillon powder)
1 thick slice of white bread, torn into pieces (or 4 tbsp fresh breadcrumbs): do not use brown bread as the soup will have bits in it
75ml single cream (plus extra, to serve, if you like)
sea salt and freshly ground black pepper

METHOD

Melt the butter in a large saucepan over a medium heat, and then add the mushrooms, cooking gently. When the mushroom juices start to run, add the parsley, garlic and nutmeg and continue to cook. Keep an eye on the heat: you may wish to turn it down so the juices don't evaporate.

Heat the stock in a separate pan.

Add the bread to the stock, and then pour over the mushrooms. Cook for 10 minutes, then blend in the pan with a stick blender (or use a goblet blender).

Gently heat the cream to a simmer in the now-empty stock pan, then add to the soup.

Adjust seasoning to taste. If I'm serving guests, I like to add a swirl of cream over the back of a spoon and a final dusting of chopped parsley.

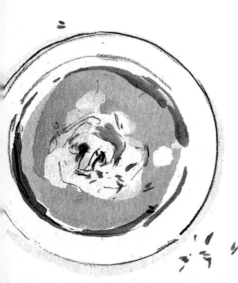

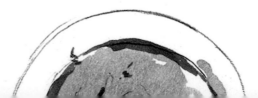

LETTUCE SOUP

I know the idea of this might sound a little odd, but do bear with me. I came up with my version because I have neither a bunny rabbit nor a compost heap at home (London apartments not being known for their vast gardens), and I was fed up with throwing away the outside leaves of those lovely, floppy English lettuces.

The soup takes about 15 minutes to make, tops, and tastes rather like a fresh, light pea soup. It's super-healthy, delicious and astonishingly frugal.

I found that the outside leaves of two lettuces made sufficient for four people for supper and a bit left over. Of course you can use a whole lettuce for this, especially if you are making a quantity of soup. (It's also worth noting that lettuces have much more abundant outer leaves in the summer.) Try Cos or little gem. Or a mixture. Whatever floats your lettuce boat.

SECRET
Add a cup of defrosted petits pois or garden peas, to thicken and add a little more flavour. Sorrel would be nice to add to the lettuce, or mint, if you go down the pea route.

SERVES 4 GENEROUSLY

1 onion, finely chopped
splash of olive oil
25g butter
1 litre chicken or vegetable stock (or enough to cover lettuce)
1 whole lettuce (or the outside leaves of 2)
sea salt and freshly ground black pepper
single cream, crème fraîche or sour cream, to serve (optional)

MFTHOD

Sauté the onion in a little olive oil and the butter, over a low heat, for at least 10 – probably 15 – minutes. You don't want it to colour at all, but you do want it properly softened. Don't attempt to speed up the process as you will burn the onion.

Meanwhile, heat the vegetable stock.

Throw the lettuce leaves, washed and all torn up, in with the onion and pour over the hot stock, to cover the leaves. Bubble away until the leaves are completely softened, then blend with a stick or goblet blender.

Add more hot stock if the soup is too thick. If you accidentally add too much liquid, simmer until it reduces to the required consistency. Season with salt and black pepper.

If you were feeling all fancy, you could add a swirl of cream, or crème fraîche, or sour cream.

ASPARAGUS RISOTTO WITH PEA PURÉE

I first came across the idea of adding a vegetable purée to a risotto at Bar Blanc in Manhattan's West Village that was round the corner from my apartment. It adds a lovely depth and colour, especially if you use peas, as the green swirls through the dish, adding an extra grassy hit and green colour.

SERVES 4 AS A MAIN OR 6 AS A SIDE DISH

2 fat bunches asparagus
100g petits pois
75g butter
approx. 1–1.6 litres vegetable stock
sea salt and freshly ground black pepper
1 small onion or a couple of shallots, finely chopped
400g risotto rice (I prefer Carnaroli)
50ml white wine or vermouth

To finish
150g Parmesan, finely grated
30g fridge-cold butter

METHOD

Fill a saucepan with about 2 cups of water and bring to the boil. Prep the asparagus by breaking off the ends where they naturally snap. Place the trimmed stalks in a steamer basket above the pan of boiling water, and add the snapped-off ends into the water itself. The trimmed stalks should be cooked al dente – do not let them get soft. (This will only take a few minutes.) Leave the ends simmering away until they're well cooked.

Cut the tips off the stalks and set aside as a garnish. Cut the remaining asparagus stalks in half. Reserve half, slice the rest into tiny rounds and set aside.

Turn off the heat under the simmering asparagus ends, fish them out and discard. DO NOT THROW AWAY THE WATER: you will use it to make the risotto later.

Blend the batch of halved asparagus stalks, petits pois, 25g of the butter, 100ml of the stock, plus a spoonful of the asparagus cooking water to a pale green purée using a stick blender or food processor. Taste and season with salt and black pepper. Set aside.

To make the risotto, gently sweat the chopped onion or shallots in the remaining butter over a low-medium heat. When the onion has softened (10 minutes or so), add the rice (it should sizzle as it hits the pan) and the white wine or vermouth.

Cook the alcohol until it has all been absorbed by the rice, stirring to make sure it does not catch, and then add a ladle of the stock (including the asparagus cooking water too) at a time. Add more stock as the previous ladle gets absorbed by the rice. Stir, stir all the time so the rice doesn't catch. It takes a while, about 20 minutes, but it's so worth the effort. I recommend the radio in the background, with a glass of the wine used for the risotto in one hand and a wooden spoon in the other. Add the little asparagus rounds about 5 minutes before the risotto is ready.

To finish, beat in the Parmesan and butter with a wooden spoon. This is the *mantecare* stage, a vital element of risotto making which ensures a glossy, smooth finish. Check the seasoning. It'll probably need lots more salt and black pepper. Just before serving, warm the asparagus purée in a small pan, then stir it in so it streaks the risotto. Garnish each plate with the reserved asparagus tips.

JERUSALEM ARTICHOKES WITH PEAS, LEMON AND GARLIC BUTTER

I adore Jerusalem artichokes but I may as well be up front about their, er, little surprise. They aren't known as 'fartichokes' for nothing. Do not serve these to anyone on a first date unless you really want to make an impression.

They aren't actually artichokes, but the tubers of a member of the sunflower family, which is why they are known as 'sunchokes' in America. Although the little, knobbly tubers can look intimidating, they are prepared in the same way as a potato. Peel and chop: done.

Whilst they make the most delicious velvety soups and purées, they are also excellent when, as here, steamed and then fried: the outside goes crunchy, giving way to a soft, yielding middle, which contrasts wonderfully with the pop of the peas. I use petits pois in this dish as they are sweeter and have a thinner skin.

SERVES 6 AS A MAIN OR 8 AS A SIDE DISH

500g Jerusalem artichokes, peeled and cut into 1cm chunks
500g petits pois
1 lemon
2 generous tbsp olive or rapeseed oil
2 fat garlic cloves, finely chopped
100g butter

SECRET
Don't be tempted to skip the steaming stage. I've tried doing this: the artichokes take at least 45 minutes to cook from raw in a frying pan.

METHOD

Steam the artichokes over a large pan of boiling water for approximately 10–15 minutes until they are al dente. (If you don't have a steamer, simply boil them.)

Whilst the artichokes are cooking, put the (frozen) peas in a bowl (preferably a metal one) and pour boiling water over them so that they start to defrost. Set aside.

Peel the entire lemon, either using a zester or a small, sharp knife to produce very thin strips of peel. Then cut the lemon in half and squeeze out the juice into a small bowl, making sure the pips are removed.

When the artichokes are done, pour the oil into a large frying pan (preferably one with high sides) placed over a medium-high heat.

Fry the artichokes for around 20 minutes until they are crispy on all sides. (Resist the temptation to keep moving them around, as this will stop them crisping.)

Drain the peas and add them to the pan with the lemon zest, garlic, butter and 1 tbsp lemon juice. Cook for a further 5 minutes before serving.

Wonderful FARMERS' MARKETS & PRODUCE SUPPLIERS

When I am travelling it is always a treat to stay in places where I can cook for myself, whether in a youth hostel (my favourite is the Hi-Marin Headlands, a few miles from the Golden Gate Bridge), a friend's home or a self-catering home (St Mawes Retreats in Cornwall are my favourites). That means I have a useful list of markets around the US and UK that I have shopped from on my travels.

SANTA MONICA FARMERS' MARKET, LOS ANGELES

The Central California coast is the fruit and vegetable bowl of America, and some of that produce ends up here: strawberries, piles of unwaxed lemons, fennel waving luxuriant fronds, oranges that smell more orange-y than an English person could think possible.

THE FERRY BUILDING, SAN FRANCISCO

Inside the building are shops, run by independent producers (favourites include Cowgirl Creamery, Acme Bread and Far West Fungi), but on Tuesday, Thursday and Saturday the justifiably famous market is open outside. You can buy fruit, vegetables, herbs, flowers, meats and eggs from small regional farmers and ranchers, many of them certified organic.

UNION SQUARE GREENMARKET, MANHATTAN, NEW YORK

An obvious inclusion, but no less wonderful for all that, and easily accessible for visitors to the city, as well as locals. With 140 regional farmers, fishermen and bakers, the open air Greenmarket is where many of the city's chefs source the ingredients for their seasonal specials – and it's where I did much of my produce shopping when I lived nearby in the East Village. Look out for New York obsessions like spring-time ramps (wild leeks), and don't miss the delicious local artisan cheese stalls. Open Monday, Wednesday, Friday and Saturday.

DELICIOUS ORCHARDS, COLT'S NECK, NEW JERSEY

Imagine my glee when I discovered I was living a few miles down the road from Jersey's most famous produce store! It's not a farmers' market, but rather a giant hangar selling almost every kind of fresh produce imaginable. Yes, it does ship in fruit and vegetables from all over the US, but it also sells great heaps of local produce, including justly renowned Jersey tomatoes, sweetcorn and apples. Don't miss the photogenic displays of squashes and gourds around Halloween (or the hot apple donuts).

THE TRURO FARMERS' MARKET, CORNWALL

Each Wednesday and Sunday, local producers gather on Lemon Quay to sell some of Cornwall's most delicious offerings. Pedigree pork from Redruth, wild game, Cornish honey and local vegetables are all available.

THE FIFTEEN SPRING AND AUTUMN FARMERS' MARKET, WATERGATE BAY, CORNWALL

Held twice a year in the main car park, you can find fresh fish, local meat, storecupboard chutneys, artisan cheeses and bread, as well as cookery demonstrations from local chefs. (I even had a pasta lesson in a tent there once.)

PARLIAMENT HILL FARMERS' MARKET

My local market in North London takes place in a school playground just on the edge of Hampstead Heath, which means I can pick up free-range eggs, a Sunday joint, and delicious bread on the way back from walking the hound.

NEWCASTLE CITY CENTRE FARMERS' MARKET

Held outdoors by the towering Grey's Monument on the first Friday of every month, all products on the market must be raised, grown or produced within a 50-mile radius of the site of the market in order to support local farmers, growers and producers.

FOOD FOR THE GREAT OUTDOORS

Until I spent time in California, my idea of hell was to be rousted out of bed for a two-hour hike. However beautiful the surroundings, I'd have pleaded an imaginary knee injury, stayed in bed, and worked my way through room service.

I never used to be like this. I did the Duke of Edinburgh's Bronze and Gold Awards at high school, which involved camping, orienteering and strenuous two- or four-day hikes over the North York Moors.

On my gap year I powered up, through and down 12 kilometres of interior rainforest to cross Pulau Tioman in Malaysia, in 90-per-cent humidity. But, once I started university, I reverted to my natural state: prone in bed with a novel.

The first inkling I had that I could enjoy exercise in adult life was when I bought a bike in London. Gradually my tentative five-minute outings became half-day expeditions down the London canal paths. Then I moved to Manhattan, bought another bicycle and became one of those boring cycling evangelists. (Yes, it's so much quicker; yes, you can bike in four-inch stilettos.)

Bicycling has taught me not to be scared of exercise; that I am naturally capable of not collapsing after five minutes of exertion; that it was just exercising in a group, where I thought people were judging my inadequacies and malcoordination, that I loathed. And that gym and games were the work of the devil.

So that brings me to California and to hiking. My dear friend, Judy, forced me up the Santa Lucia mountains and I loved every minute and became one of those slightly tedious, outdoor evangelists.

And, of course, given that I think about food all the time, I started to think about the kind of food I wanted to eat both when I was on the hoof, and when I was picnicking: because half the fun of a hike is the food stop.

I am always quite surprised when I read suggestions for outdoor food that involve great efforts of assembly; or multiple containers; or messy, sticky foods. The first just seems like hard work, the second too heavy, and the last a magnet for wasps and other creepy-crawlies.

What I want on a picnic or a hike are simple foods that taste delicious in the open air, don't dribble down your arm and don't require the culinary skills of a chef to assemble. I'm also not very keen on spending hours in the kitchen making pork pies or similar – food that I can make, pack up and go out with quickly means heading outside can have an element of spontaneity.

FIVE GREAT PLACES TO GO HIKING IN

LOS ANGELES

1 TOPANGA STATE PARK (for the uphill workout – and the views)
2 WILL ROGERS STATE PARK (for the views of the Pacific Ocean)
3 RUNYON CANYON (because it's hard to believe you are in Hollywood)
4 CHARLIE TURNER TRAIL. GRIFFITH PARK (for the Downtown Los Angeles skyline view)
5 VASQUEZ ROCKS (because they have shot Star Trek TV episodes here)

THREE SANDWICHES
TO EAT ON THE HOOF
WHICH DON'T DRIP DOWN YOUR ARM

I never cease to be astonished at the sandwiches that
I see suggested for outdoor activities. The last thing
anyone wants is a messy lunch that dribbles everywhere
and which, if left untouched, starts to smell.

So, for that reason, I am a big fan of mashing my
sandwich fillings, so that nothing can fall out. Another
great trick is to use rolls from which you have hollowed
out some of the bread, so that the filling can sit securely
inside the crust. Pitta is also good for this, as you can
spread a filling inside without it oozing out of the sides.

FETA, HERB AND ROASTED TOMATO IN ROLLS
Once I've scooped out some of the inside of a wholemeal
roll, I like to fill it with a combination of mashed feta
and roasted or sun-dried tomatoes that have been finely
chopped, along with some green herbs – chives are great.

CHEESE AND PICKLE ON GRANARY
One of my favourite sandwiches, but slices of cheese can
easily slide out of your sandwich due to the emollient
quality of the pickle. So, I suggest grating the cheese
(about 50g per sandwich) and binding it with 1 teaspoon
mayonnaise. Spread one side of the inside of the bread with
pickle – avoid the lumps, or use a smooth chutney – and the
other with your grated cheese and mayo. Press firmly down
to seal the sandwich together.

CREAM CHEESE AND HAM IN PETITS PAINS
Mash together 1 tablespoon cream cheese and a slice of ham
that you have rolled up and then cut into tiny pieces. Hollow
out the petits pains and stuff the mixture inside, being
careful not to overfill.

AND ONE EXTRA IDEA, FOR AVOCADO FANS
This is not the sandwich to make for a long hike, but it's
great to eat an hour or so after having been made. Simply
scoop out the flesh from an avocado and mash it with some
salt and a squeeze of lemon juice to stop it discolouring.
Then, finely chop together a few sprigs of watercress and
a spring onion, and mix with the avocado. This mixture is
great in granary rolls and, again, I suggest removing some of
the crumb to allow the filling to stay securely inside the roll.

CLIMPING, WEST SUSSEX

In the winter this feels like one of the windiest beaches I've visited, but in summer the shingle means that it isn't quite as busy as other beaches nearby and, so long as you take a comfy blanket, it's perfect for a picnic (no sand in your sandwiches).

MAWGAN PORTH, CORNWALL

Not as popular as some Cornish beaches, this quiet and sandy bay, some five miles north of Newquay, is particularly good for a brisk dog-walk very early in the morning. It's equally popular with my sand-castle-building godchildren as it is with the older surfers. I also recommend a brisk, ten-minute haul up to the cliff top to watch the sunset.

CAMBER SANDS, EAST SUSSEX

Possibly Britain's best sandy beach, this was our favourite family expedition as children. Wonderful for sunbathing, this beach offers plenty to do — and there's easy access to ice creams for afters, too.

MY FAVOURITE BRITISH BEACHES FOR A PICNIC

CLEY NEXT THE SEA, NORFOLK

My best friend Emma's mother says that Cley reminds her of Texas, where she grew up: on a perfect summer day it has the same feeling of big blue skies and limitless horizons. Another shingly beach, it can be a bracingly breezy place to sit even in the summer, but if you take a windbreak and anchor it well, it is a glorious spot for a picnic.

BAMBURGH CASTLE BEACH, NORTHUMBERLAND

I went to Newcastle University, and when academic pressures got to us, we would drive up the coast to Bamburgh to picnic on the sands. Known for its beautiful views towards the Farne Islands, its abundant birdlife (look out for the oystercatchers) and its clean water, this is one of the North East's best beaches.

GREENAWAY BEACH, CORNWALL

A blissful, dogs-welcome, coarse-sand beach, tucked up to the north of the family-friendly Daymer Bay. You can't swim here: it's all rock pools, which my sausage dog finds irresistible.

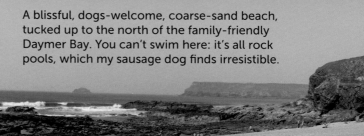

It's often completely deserted, partly because it's a ten-minute walk from the nearest parking and there is a steep, often waterlogged and slippery set of rock-hewn steps down to the beach.

GRANOLA BARS

I'm afraid that it is a complete fallacy that these are a healthy alternative to sweets. Granola bars may be full of things that are good (or better) for you, like low-glycaemic-index carbs, seeds and nuts, but they are always bound together with something sticky; and whether it's agave or honey, it's still a sugar. That being said, if given a choice between a nutrition-free chocolate bar or one of these delicious snacks, I'd go for the squirrel-friendly one every time.

I've experimented a lot with these – you don't want a super-crumbly bar when you're hiking, so make sure you press them very firmly into the pan before baking. If in doubt, they always benefit from a longer cooking time in the oven than a shorter one.

MAKES 12
200g porridge oats
100g butter, plus extra for greasing
25ml cooking oil (rapeseed is best)
3 tbsp honey or agave nectar
1 tbsp golden syrup
50g light muscovado sugar
100g sunflower seeds
35g sesame seeds
35g pumpkin seeds
20g linseeds (optional)
½ tbsp ground linseeds (optional)
50g almonds, chopped
20 x 20cm square baking tin

VARIATIONS
You could add 50g chocolate chips to the mixture if you have a sweeter tooth. Coconut flakes and little bits of dried apple are good, too.

METHOD
Preheat the oven to 180°C/350°F/gas mark 4.

Scatter the oats over a baking tray and toast in the oven for 25 minutes.

Place the butter and oil in a large saucepan and heat until the butter has melted. Add the rest of the liquid ingredients with the sugar and combine. Remove from the heat the moment the sugar has dissolved.

Grease the baking tin and line it either with greaseproof paper or a silicone baking sheet. Make sure that it sticks up over the side of the tin so that you can lift out the granola mix when it is cooked.

Add all the dry ingredients to a large bowl, mix together, then pour over the hot oil and syrup and stir thoroughly to combine. Spoon the mixture into the baking tin and press it very firmly down.

Bake for 25 minutes. Keep an eye on it: when the edges look brown it is done.

Leave it in the tin for 5 minutes to cool and then turn out onto a chopping board. Immediately cut it into 12 pieces with a very sharp knife; if you leave this process until it is cold you won't be able to cut it without it crumbling.

Keep in an airtight tin.

SHAKE-IT-UP SALADS IN JARS

These are a big thing amongst my friends in California, who will take any opportunity to eat outdoors, but don't want to lug a formal picnic around with them.

One of the biggest pains about picnicking is the need to pack things in lots of separate jars and bottles so that food doesn't get soggy, waterlogged or floppy en route. Jar salads solve this problem because the dressing or sauce sits in the bottom of the jar, with the rest of the salad layered over the top, so that until you shake it up – or tip it out – nothing gets mixed together. There's also much less chance of your dressing leaking as there is only a small amount in each jar. Even if the lid becomes unscrewed, the other ingredients should soak it up before there is a chance of spillage. The only requirement is to keep the jar upright. To be honest, these are more of a car thing than a hiking thing: carrying a glass jar around is risky and heavy, but I think of them as the perfect parking-lot lunch before a hike.

American Mason jars and British Kilner jars are the ideal containers. But, really, any large jar with a secure lid will do, unless you are mad keen on Instagramming your lunch. (Make sure you sterilise the jars before filling them by putting them in a hot dishwasher or filling them with boiling water.)

The basic rule is dressing first (don't forget to season it), then the heaviest ingredients. Choose the ones that are least likely to soak up the sauce first, with leaves and herbs at the top.

MEXICAN
Avocado and lemon dressing
Chicken
Black beans
Sweetcorn
Tomato
Lettuce

CHICKEN
Lemon vinaigrette
Chicken
Cannellini beans
Tomato
Watercress-and-rocket salad

GREEK
Olive oil dressing with oregano
Feta cheese
Olives
Cucumber
Tomato
Romaine lettuce

CHICKEN NOODLE
Soy and rice vinegar dressing
Chicken
Rice noodles
Beansprouts
Lettuce

GOAT'S CHEESE AND CHICKPEA
Olive oil and balsamic dressing
Goat's cheese
Chickpeas
Bulgur wheat
Tomato
Rocket

TRAIL MIX FOR JOANNA

When I was 17, Joanna and I got lost on the North York Moors for five hours on our Duke of Edinburgh's Gold Expedition Challenge. It was Easter: raining, cold and muddy, but we got through our navigational challenges (in the days of flapping, wet maps and misted-over compasses) by singing the entire Smiths back catalogue, and alternately eating Creme Eggs and trail mix.

For those who don't hike, trail mix is a mix of nuts, dried fruit and, sometimes, grains and sweets, which is intended to boost energy. There's no consensus on how it came into existence, although my 17-year-old self was charmed by the discovery that Ray and Japhy in Jack Kerouac's novel, *The Dharma Bums*, ate trail mix.

There's no hard-and-fast rule for the making of trail mix: I just lob in all the things I think I might like to chew on as I tramp up hill and down dale. I do try to avoid adding chocolates and sweets: slow-release carbs like nuts are infinitely more useful to the hiker. I'm also going to admit that I make up trail mix to keep me going during fashion week season when, with maybe 12 shows a day to see, there is no time to sit down to eat, and on-the-hoof munching is what keeps me moving forward.

MY PERFECT MIX IS:
pumpkin seeds
sunflower seeds
dried apple pieces, broken into
 chunks
dried cranberries
dried apricots, cut into quarters
almonds
cashews
hazelnuts

CARB-DODGING MINI QUICHES

I'm rather pleased with these little puffy egg things. They are basically a quiche mixture without pastry or cream, which means they are perfect for picnics and outdoors, as there are no crumbly bits to spill down your front. They're also pretty good if you are carb-dodging.

MAKES 6
butter or cooking spray, for greasing
2 large eggs
25g cheese (I use Parmesan or Cheddar)
4 spring onions
lots of black pepper and a pinch of sea salt
handful chopped green soft herbs
6-hole cupcake tin

METHOD
Preheat the oven to 180°C/350°F/gas mark 4. Either wipe a little butter around each hole in the cupcake tin or, if you're in a particularly diet-minded mood, use cooking spray.

Then, to produce 6 of these, beat the eggs together and grate in the cheese, using the finest grater you have (a little goes further this way).

Chop the spring onions, including most of the green, and mix together with the egg and herbs, along with lots of black pepper and a pinch of salt.

Divide the mixture between the cupcake holes. It should half-fill each one. Pop into the hot oven and cook for about 10 minutes until they are all puffed up like mini Yorkshire puddings.

They will deflate as they cool, but they still taste just as good.

VARIATIONS
25g of any of the following can also be added: chopped ham, cooked mushrooms, cooked leeks or onions.

GOOD THINGS IN THERMOS FLASKS

The discovery of wide-necked Thermos flasks was a revelation to me. I'd tried putting chunky soups in a standard flask, but something always got stuck inside and you certainly couldn't put anything that wasn't liquid in them.

The possibility of a wide-necked flask suddenly means that picnics can get a lot more exciting, so you no longer need to trail endless boxes and bags to create something delicious on site. As long as you prep your flask properly first by warming it with boiling water, whatever you put in should stay warm all day.

Hot food needn't be restricted to winter picnics or sitting in the car at a point-to-point in the countryside. My favourite things to add are baby new potatoes with a good knob of butter, some sea salt and mint. They go particularly well with quiches and with salads. Petits pois prepped the same way are excellent, too.

That being said, the following recipes from this book are perfect for putting in a flask:

- **Courgette and Pea Orzotto (page 76)**
- **Winter-Warming Beef, Barley, Mushroom and Carrot Stew (page 41)**
- **Pork, Chorizo and White Bean Stew (page 42)**
- **Mushroom Soup for Mushroom-ophobes (page 102)**

Do think hard about including pastas in sauces, and starches that might continue to absorb liquid and thus go soggy. Barley is bombproof, so it will keep its shape; risotto rice will not.

JEWELLED JELLIES
IN JARS

What a lovely thing to take on smart picnics: I'm thinking outdoor theatre or concerts in the summer, where something a little more elegant than a package of sandwiches is called for. (However, best not to attempt these in a heatwave, unless you particularly like drinking your jelly.)

I use a product called Vege-Gel (derived from seaweed and widely available) to set these, rather than gelatine. I don't like the smell of the latter when it is cooking and I don't see the point when a perfectly good alternative is available. It also means you don't have to worry about any vegetarians in the alfresco group.

Adhering to my no-faff mantra, these are very quick to make, and to set – they are firm in about 45 minutes. You do need to make the jelly in layers – don't worry, these won't show when they set – as, otherwise, all the fruit floats to the top.

MAKES 4–6 LITTLE JELLIES

500ml cold water
70ml elderflower cordial
1 sachet vegetarian gel powder
(I recommend Vege-Gel)
2 handfuls berries to set in the
jelly; I've used blueberries
and raspberries
4–6 little preserving or screw-
top jars

METHOD

Pour the cold water and elderflower cordial into a saucepan and sprinkle the gel powder on top. Mix carefully and bring slowly to boiling point.

Whilst the mixture is heating, place a few berries in each of the jars. When the jelly has boiled, carefully pour it to just cover the first layer of fruit.

Allow this first layer to set, then reheat the remaining jelly to liquidity again, drop in some more berries and, again, cover them with jelly. Repeat as many times as necessary to fill the jar – I try to aim for 3 layers.

These will set in about 45 minutes, but I do recommend keeping in the fridge overnight to ensure a firm set.

> ### SECRET
> Don't be tempted to use sliced strawberries: they leach their colour into the jelly.

SWEET THINGS

When I was a little girl, I was fascinated by the Cordon Bleu series of cookbooks, with their navy-blue and white covers. There were two in particular: one called *Hot Puddings* and one called *Cold Desserts*.

Hot Puddings intrigued me because it did, after all, contain sugar, chocolate and other ingredients appealing to the infant mind.

But as much as I love a hot pudding (more on this later), it was *Cold Desserts* that exercised an almost mystic thrall over me. I used to gaze lovingly at the meringue concoctions, glasses of trifles, lavish use of whipped cream, and luscious strawberries that appeared on almost every page.

Although I obsessively bookmarked them with scraps of paper, I don't remember either myself or my mother actually cooking from them. Those desserts were from the realms of fantasy, not reality.

As an adult, re-reading those books awakened my love of desserts and puddings, but it didn't instil any desire to spend hours in the kitchen wielding a piping bag or constructing complicated choux towers.

Instead, my taste runs towards a simpler approach: one where you can cook ahead, or serve up a large bowl or platter, into which everyone can dive.

My presentation may be simple, but there has been no compromise elsewhere: I feel strongly that if you are simplifying the processes, then the ingredients must be excellent in themselves and that there is no excuse for serving an unattractive plate of food. It's wonderful how a sprinkle of icing sugar, a grating of chocolate, or a few mint leaves can perk up a dish. That being said, no artful smears, towers or unnecessary sauces, please.

On those occasions where you want a bit of warmth and comfort, you can't beat a hot pudding. There are so many occasions where it's the perfect end to a meal: a long, leisurely Sunday lunch in winter; supper around the kitchen table with friends; or when you just want to dive headfirst into some comfort food. There is something intensely reassuring about them, maybe because we ate them so often in school dinners, or as children.

Hot puddings are often simple to make: there's no waiting around for mousses to set, or ice cream to harden, and just because a pudding is served warm doesn't mean you need to make it there and then: you can either prepare in advance and pop in the oven when you serve the main course, or you can cook the entire thing beforehand and just reheat it.

I'm including some squidgy, fruit-packed cakes here because I think they are underutilised at the end of a meal: cake isn't just for tea, and whipping up a cake batter can be a lot quicker than constructing a pud from scratch.

Traditionalists will want custard with their pudding (or maybe *crème anglaise* if they are feeling fancy). But don't forget the appeal of clotted cream; dense, decadent spoons of Jersey cream; or silky-smooth vanilla ice cream – all of these bring a wonderful, cool contrast to the steamy sweetness of a hot pud.

MIXED BERRY SUMMER PUDDING

It took me a Very Long Time to get my head around summer pudding: I thought the idea of fruit-juice-soaked soggy bread utterly revolting. Then I needed to knock up a pud for a last-minute lunch and all I had in the house was a loaf of good white bread and several punnets of berries. Clearly, a summer pudding was the solution. Because I couldn't bear to watch other people eat and deprive myself, I tentatively forked up a mouthful.

Reader, I loved it. Somehow, the bread doesn't taste soggy, so much as just saturated with fruit.

Traditionally, a summer pudding contains just raspberries and redcurrants, but I added both blackcurrants and resolutely non-traditional blueberries, which I think add a little texture, as well as relief from the sharpness of the currants. One should not be tempted to try using strawberries here (they just turn to mush). And really, this is not the time to use up forgotten berries – summer pudding is designed to show off perfect summer fruit, so use the best you can find.

SERVES 6 GENEROUSLY

750g soft summer fruit (my favourite combination is: 100g redcurrants, 100g blackcurrants, 450g raspberries, 100g blueberries)
100g golden granulated sugar
7 medium slices of good white bread (a sandwich loaf is perfect)
thick or clotted cream, to serve
standard pudding basin

SECRET

Only use very good white bread for this – definitely not sliced bread which will turn to disgusting soggy pap after a stint soaking up juicy berries. Yuk.

METHOD

Using the tines of a fork, slide the currants off their stems, and pick over the raspberries and blueberries. Place a medium saucepan over a low heat and tip in the fruit and sugar. Cook for 5 minutes, no more, until the berries have started to release their juices.

Meanwhile, cut the crusts off the bread. Using a pastry cutter or by cutting around a small plate, cut 1 bread circle to fit the base of the pudding basin, and use this to line the bottom of the basin. Then line the sides with pieces of bread, cut to fit, making sure there are no gaps.

Remove a couple of tablespoons of the berry juice from the saucepan and reserve. Tip the fruit and its juices into the bread-lined basin and create a lid over the top using the rest of the bread.

Place a small plate over the top of the pudding and weigh it down with a tin, for example. Ideally, leave this overnight, although I have found that you can get a good result if you make this about 3 hours before serving.

When you are ready to serve it, simply slip a knife around the edge of the basin, remove the plate and replace with an upturned serving plate. Invert the basin, tap the bottom hard and, hopefully, your summer pudding will slide out onto the plate. You will inevitably find some white patches on the bread, especially if you haven't been able to leave it overnight, so spoon the reserved juice over those parts of the pudding.

Serve with thick or clotted cream, or pour lovely, thick double cream in a gentle stream over each portion.

PATRIOTIC PAVLOVA

I first made this for a Thanksgiving lunch in Los Angeles where, in direct contradiction of urban legend, people do eat both cream and sugar. Especially when it looks as pretty as this.

I was scared by the idea of making pavlovas for years: I always thought the meringue would break, that it was all far, far too complicated. That is, until I realised that this is not only very simple and quick to make, but can be done the night before, which dramatically decreases stress in the kitchen. You do need a hand-held electric whisk or stand mixer both for the egg whites and for the cream – unless, of course, you particularly want to spend half the day with a hand whisk.

If raspberries and blueberries do not appeal, there are plenty of other toppings that work beautifully on a pavlova. Sliced nectarines and raspberries are a lovely combination in the summer, as are plums and flaked almonds in the colder months.

SERVES 6–8
4 egg whites
pinch of salt
225g white sugar
1 tsp white wine vinegar
1 heaped tsp cornflour
1 tsp vanilla extract
300ml double cream
1 punnet raspberries
1 punnet blueberries
icing sugar, for dusting
  (optional)

METHOD
Preheat the oven to 180°C/350°F/gas mark 4 and line a baking tray either with baking parchment or, better still, a silicone baking sheet. (This will also decrease stress, as the meringue just slips off and minimises any chance of breakage.)

Tip the egg whites and salt into a scrupulously clean, dry mixing bowl, or the bowl of a stand mixer. Beat with a hand-held electric whisk or the mixer until the egg whites are super-fluffy (the stiff white should not drop off the whisk), but do be careful not to overbeat as they will start to separate. Then, keeping the whisk running, add the sugar a spoonful at a time.

Then whisk the vinegar, cornflour and vanilla into the glossy mixture as quickly as you can.

Using a large spoon, heap the meringue mixture onto the baking tray in a rough oval, making a slight depression in the middle, which will hold the fruit later.

Turn the oven down to 150°C/300°F/gas mark 2 and bake the meringue for 45 minutes.

When the cooking time is up, turn off the oven and leave the meringue inside to cool. (I usually make this the evening before and leave it in there overnight.)

Very carefully remove the meringue from the tray, peeling off the liner as you go, and slide onto your serving dish. Do check that the dish is big enough, as meringue is too delicate to overhang and will break, as I found out to my cost.

Just before serving whip the cream but do not leave it whirring away as you do something else, as the difference between lovely, light and floppy, and solid cheese-y cream is a second of inattention. Generally the cream will be whipped before it looks done, so keep checking.

Spread the cream over the meringue.

Pick over the fruit and then tip it randomly over the cream. Some sifted icing sugar looks pretty, if you like.

THE BROADWAY PANHANDLER, MANHATTAN, NEW YORK

Just below Union Square, and a few blocks from Strand Bookstore (see page 58) and its excellent cookery section, this is, hands down, my favourite cookshop in the world. It's not so big that you become overwhelmed or so small that they have over-edited their stock: there is just enough of anything you might possibly need in your kitchen.

Whether I am seeking a very particular size in metallic cupcake cases or a new kitchen apron, this store is always my first port of call. It also has a very serious selection of knives and offers a sharpening service too.

65 East 8th Street, New York, NY 10003

BLACKBERRY AND APPLE TRIFLE

My grandfather loved trifle so my mother always made him a proper English trifle from scratch, layering up pieces of homemade whisked sponge, liberally soaked with sherry and spread with jam, fresh fruit, *crème anglaise* and a drift of whipped cream, garnished with flaked almonds.

My version is a more modern take, but don't worry: it still sticks to the traditional trinity of custard, cream and sponge. I just prefer to use a *crème pâtissière* as it is much thicker, creating a separate custard layer, rather than oozing through the entire pudding.

Instead of sherry I use the delicious French blackberry liqueur, *crème de mûre*, which really brings out the blackberry flavour of the pud, although you could happily substitute more easily available *crème de cassis* – or revert to sherry if that is what you have. There's no need to be prescriptive with a trifle. (If you are booze-free, you can use apple juice instead.)

I'm afraid that I don't make my trifle sponges: I have discovered that shop-bought Madeira cake is perfect. It's dense enough not to go soggy and tastes wonderful when saturated with booze.

In winter I make the trifle with a packet of frozen fruits of the forest – frozen blackberries are almost impossible to find, and fruits of the forest are a very successful substitute.

The key to not being stressed by a trifle is to remember that it is really a series of separate ingredients, piled together in a very deep glass dish, most of which can be prepared the day before if necessary.

SERVES 8–10

Crème Pâtissière (see opposite)
2 quantities Apple Sauce (see page 97)
250g frozen or fresh blackberries
squeeze of lemon juice and 1 dsp sugar, if using fresh blackberries
approx. 450g shop-bought Madeira cake
50ml crème de mûre (or crème de cassis, or apple juice)
5 tbsp good blackberry jam (e.g. Fresh Blackberry Jam, see page 146)
570ml double cream
100g flaked almonds

METHOD

First make the Crème Pâtissière so that it has time to cool. Then make the Apple Sauce, leaving some pieces whole, and allow to cool.

Defrost the fruit if using frozen, setting a few berries aside to decorate. If using fresh fruit, set some aside, then tip into a pan with a squeeze of lemon juice and 1 dsp sugar. When the sugar has dissolved, remove from the heat and allow to cool.

Cut the Madeira cake into mini slabs about the length of your middle finger and use them to line the bottom of a trifle dish or large, deep, glass serving bowl. Douse the cake with the alcohol or juice. Spread the jam over the sponge. Now pile the fruit (it must be cool) over the sponges, followed by the Apple Sauce. This gives a nice, smooth layer over which to pile the Crème Pâtissière, which goes on top next.

Now whip the cream very carefully: it is very easy to overwhip. You are aiming for a nice, floppy texture; generally it is ready before it looks it, so stop and stir it through before you think it's fully whipped. Spoon on top of the Crème Pâtissière.

Decorate the cream with the whole blackberries and scatter over the flaked almonds.

THREE GLORIOUS SHERRIES

Like so many people, my first sip of sherry came out of a blue, glass bottle and accompanied a piece of Christmas cake. It wasn't until I visited Jerez de la Frontera in Spain that I realised that sherry's variety means it can be as delicious with roast beef and cheese as it can with puddings and cake.

Fino
The driest, palest and youngest of all sherries, chilled fino is perfect with tapas, but if you travel to Jerez you will see it drunk everywhere as you would a white wine. (Beware its deceptive 15 per cent alcohol content.)

Pedro Ximénez
My absolute favourite: made from the grape of the same name, this is one of the world's oldest dessert wines. This rich, dark, sweet sherry tastes like essence of macerated raisins and is sublime poured over vanilla ice cream.

Matusalem
Produced in very small quantities, Matusalem is a dark Oloroso sherry, made from a blend of 75 per cent Palomino and 25 per cent Pedro Ximénez grapes. Aged for over 30 years, it has a rich, sweet finish, which is wonderful with strong cheeses and tastes lovely against cooked apples.

CREME PATISSIERE

500ml whole milk
1 tsp vanilla extract
4 egg yolks
6 tbsp icing sugar
4 tbsp cornflour

Heat the milk and vanilla in a pan. Meanwhile beat together the egg yolks with the icing sugar and the cornflour. When the milk is simmering, slowly dribble the egg mixture onto it, whisking away.

It will eventually thicken into perfect crème pâtissière. Scoop into a dish to cool. And that's it.

CHOCOLATE ORANGE MOUSSE

Chocolate mousse was, hands-down, my family's favourite Sunday-lunch pudding when my sister and I were little. My father loved it because he only likes dark chocolate; my sister and I because it seemed grown-up and therefore very appealing; and my mother because it was simple and quick to make.

This is not a light and fluffy mousse, but rather a dense, indulgent affair. My mother always used an Arabella Boxer recipe, from her amazing 1960s classic *First Slice Your Cookbook*. This fascinated me as a child because it was spiral-bound and cut into three separate, horizontal sections – starters, mains and puddings, so you could create a perfect three-course menu. I have adapted her recipe here.

The main thing to remember is that you need to make this in advance. It can be made the night before and popped in the fridge, but I find that if I beat this up before I put the Sunday joint in the oven, that's plenty of time for it to firm up – about two hours before serving.

SERVES 8

120g chocolate (70% cocoa solids), plus extra to decorate
4 eggs, separated
1 tbsp Cointreau or freshly squeezed orange juice
2 tsp caster sugar

METHOD

Break the chocolate into pieces and put in a heatproof bowl over, but not touching, a pan of simmering water. When the chocolate begins to melt, turn the heat off, beat the chocolate with a wooden spoon, and allow to cool.

Scoop the cooled, melted chocolate into a large mixing bowl.

Beat the egg yolks together with a fork, and stir quickly into the melted chocolate mixture, followed by the liqueur or juice.

In a scrupulously clean, dry bowl, whisk the egg whites into firm peaks: I use a stand mixer or hand-held electric whisk. (It will take forever to do this with a hand whisk or egg beater.) Then whisk in the sugar.

Whisk one-third of the egg whites into the chocolate mixture, until combined. Using a metal spoon, fold the rest of the egg white very gently into the mixture, until just combined (be careful not to overbeat).

Scoop into a pretty serving bowl and refrigerate for at least 2 hours or overnight, until set. Sprinkle over finely grated chocolate. (I like to use my grandmother's cut-glass bowl.)

INDIVIDUAL CHOCOLATE TRIFLES

These are the perfect make-ahead puds for which you need the basic
Chocolate Orange Mousse recipe opposite (leaving out the Cointreau or
juice), half a quantity of the Brownies (see page 150), as much whipped
cream as you crave, and some chocolate for grating or flaked almonds
or chopped nuts.

 For six people, split the mousse between six stemmed glasses and allow
to set (minimum two hours). Then cut the brownies into small chunks and
divide evenly among the glasses. Top with whipped cream and grate over
some chocolate.

 I use glasses for these mini trifles because I like seeing the layers of
mousse, brownie and cream, but there is no reason why you can't make
them in whatever vessels you have to hand: I've used tea cups and small
bowls before.

SUMMER BERRY TART

Whilst I've been making classic quiches for years with great success, I've always been slightly scared by the idea of making a proper pâtisserie-type tart. They require two ingredients which are notorious for going wrong: *pâte brisée* (an extremely short, buttery pastry which can be a pig to work with as, if you get it too short, it has to be pressed into place rather than rolled); and *crème pâtissière* (proper confectioner's custard which splits if you so much as look at it the wrong way).

It does not help that my mother makes extraordinarily good pastry, and thinks nothing of knocking up a tart at the last minute. Leave it to the experts I've always said, or do as the French and buy one from your local pâtisserie. So, I'd never made *pâté brisée* or *crème pâtissière* before. And, as I don't much like hot eggy runny custard, I always presumed that I didn't like *crème pâtissière*. How wrong was I? Last year I discovered that I loved it **and** that neither the *crème* nor the pastry are nearly as difficult to make as I had thought. So here you are – and what could be prettier?

SERVES 8–10

1 quantity Crème Pâtissière
  (see page 127)
berries, to decorate (I use
  approx. 300g raspberries,
  200g blueberries and 350g
  sliced strawberries)

For the pastry
250g plain flour
100g fridge-cold butter, cut into
  small pieces
1 egg yolk
50ml cold water with a pinch
  of salt
50g icing sugar
*26cm fluted tart tin, preferably
  non-stick and loose-bottomed,
  greased*
*baking beans (you can use
  lentils or rice if you don't have
  baking beans)*

METHOD

First make the Crème Pâtissière so that it has time to cool.

Throw the pastry ingredients into a food processor and pulse until it comes together, keeping an eagle eye on it so it isn't overworked.

If making by hand, place the flour in a large mixing bowl and add the butter. Using the fingertips of one hand, rub the butter into the flour until it resembles breadcrumbs. Then make a well in the middle and add the egg yolk, salted water and icing sugar. Mix together with your hands. The moment the pastry comes together, dump it onto a floured board, push into a ball, wrap in clingfilm and pop into the fridge to rest for an hour.

When you are ready to assemble the tart, preheat the oven to 180°C/350°F/gas mark 4.

Roll the rested pastry out on a floured surface using a rolling pin. It needs to be a circle slightly bigger than the tart tin. Lift the pastry loosely around the rolling pin and unroll it directly into the tin. Press it into shape, leave about 1cm over the edge and trim off any remaining overhang with a knife.

Line the pastry with greaseproof paper or baking parchment and fill with baking beans to stop the pastry rising during baking. Bake for 25–35 minutes, depending on your oven. Allow the pastry to cool slightly before removing the beans on their paper and gently popping the pastry shell out of the tin and onto a wire rack to cool. Using a sharp knife, trim the overhanging pastry around the edges.

When the pastry shell is cold, tip in and spread out the crème pâtissière and spend a fun 10 minutes decorating with the berries.

CHERRY ETON MESS

When I spent the summer in New Jersey a few years ago, this was the pudding I'd make to eat outdoors, under the trees. It makes me think of long, sunny days, and friends. The combination of crushed meringues, cream and soft fruit is one that rarely fails to please.

I love making meringues: I have a passion for that dense marshmallow-y chewiness in the interior you can't get in commercial or restaurant offerings. When I was little, my mother, the ace cook, used to make the chewiest meringues in her AGA and sandwich them together with dense whipped cream for birthday parties.

That being said, Eton Mess works perfectly well with shop-bought meringues. (Buy the nicest ones you can afford.)

Strawberries are the traditional fruit in an Eton Mess, but I have a few other suggestions.

> ## SECRET
> If you're the kind of person who likes marshmallow-y meringues, leave them to cool in the oven for only 30 minutes. For the dry-and-crispy-centred-meringue lovers out there, leave your meringues in a cooling oven for as long as possible.

SERVES 6
8 egg whites
pinch of salt
500g white sugar
2 tsp white wine vinegar
3 heaped tsp cornflour, sifted
1 tsp vanilla extract
250g cherries, pitted and halved, or one of the variations below
560ml double cream

VARIATIONS
- Mixed berries: raspberries, redcurrants, blackcurrants, blueberries
- Passionfruit and mango
- Chopped apricots and flaked almonds
- Persimmon and mint
- Strawberries and mint

METHOD
Preheat the oven to 180°C/350°F/gas mark 4 and line 2 baking trays with baking parchment.

Tip the egg whites and salt into a scrupulously clean, dry mixing bowl, or the bowl of a stand mixer. Beat with a hand-held electric whisk or the mixer until the egg whites are super-fluffy (the stiff white should not drop off the whisk), but do be careful not to overbeat as they will start to separate. Then, keeping the whisk running, add the sugar a spoonful at a time.

Then whisk the vinegar, cornflour and vanilla into the glossy mixture as quickly as you can.

Heap large spoonfuls of the meringue mixture onto the baking trays, turn the oven down to 150°C/300°F/gas mark 2 and bake for 30 minutes.

When the cooking time is up, turn off the oven and leave the meringues inside to cool for 30–60 minutes.

You can serve this either piled onto a large platter for everyone to help themselves, or you can divide into individual bowls. I sometimes use vintage tea cups.

Pull the meringues into chunks.

Whip the double cream to soft peaks using a hand-held electric whisk or a balloon whisk (and a lot of elbow grease). Spoon the cream and meringue chunks into the platter or cups and tip the cherries over.

WARM APPLE AND HAZELNUT STREUSEL CAKE

I first made this cake when I discovered a package of hazelnut flour from the New York deli, Dean & Deluca, languishing in the back of my kitchen cupboard. Upon further investigation it turned out to be a fancy name for ground hazelnuts and I thought they would be perfect in a cake with apples, as ground nuts add a lovely, squidgy quality.

   Whilst it eats beautifully cold as a picnic cake wrapped in greaseproof paper, I do think this cake comes into its own in the winter months as a pudding, served warm from the oven, with a blanket of either cold double cream or silky egg custard.

   I think slightly tarter dessert apples like Cox's Orange Pippin are best here. It's also a fantastic way to use up those slightly past-it apples in the fruit bowl. If you can't lay your hands on ground hazelnuts, then this cake works just as beautifully with ground almonds.

SERVES 8–10
225g butter, softened, plus extra for greasing
450g apples
juice of ½ lemon
175g caster sugar
50g soft brown sugar
1 tsp vanilla extract
3 eggs
225g self-raising flour
2 tsp baking powder
1 tsp ground cinnamon
30g ground hazelnuts
icing sugar, to serve

For the streusel topping
2 tbsp ground hazelnuts
2 tbsp soft brown sugar
1 tbsp melted butter
1 tsp ground cinnamon
deep, 20cm springform cake tin

METHOD

Preheat the oven to 180°C/350°F/gas mark 4.

I'm a big fan of reusable silicone tin liners, which mean you don't need to grease or line your tin. If you don't have a silicone liner, grease the cake tin and line the sides and base with greaseproof paper or baking parchment. (This cake will really stick otherwise.)

Peel, core and chop the apples into 1cm chunks. To stop them going brown, pour the lemon juice over and mix together.

You can do this next bit by hand but, seriously, unless you are looking for ways to incorporate exercise into every moment of your daily routine, I highly recommend a food processor or electric mixer. Put the butter and both sugars into a stand mixing bowl and beat together. You are aiming for a light and fluffy mixture.

Add the vanilla and then 1 egg at a time, along with a spoonful of flour – this will prevent the mixture curdling.

Mix together the baking powder, cinnamon and ground hazelnuts with the rest of the flour and add to the cake one heaped spoonful at a time, being careful to stop beating the moment the flour has been incorporated. (Overbeating will lead to a heavier cake.)

If using a food processor, scoop out the batter into a bowl and add the apple pieces. Fold them all together. If using a stand or hand mixer, just add the apples to the mixing bowl and fold together. Make sure that the apple pieces are distributed throughout the cake batter.

Don't worry if the batter is stiffer than you would want in a sponge cake. This is both because the apples will leach their juice during baking, and because you want the batter to hold the pieces otherwise they will sink to the bottom of the cake.

Spoon the batter into the lined cake tin.

Lick the cake bowl.

Make sure that the top of the cake batter is level-ish (use a spatula or the back of a spoon).

Mix together the ingredients for the streusel topping and sprinkle over the top of the cake. Don't worry about it clumping. This is good, as it will make for crunchy bits.

Pop in the oven for 45 minutes. I find that the top browns very quickly, so I add a piece of paper over the top of the cake at the 45-minute mark and then cook for a further 15 minutes to make 1 hour total.

As oven temperatures can vary, do test the cake for done-ness at 45 minutes with a skewer. If the cake is cooked, the skewer will come out clean. Test in several places around the centre of the cake, because if you hit a piece of apple the skewer will come out clean, giving a false positive. If there is any hint of batter on the skewer it needs more cooking. Check again after 5 minutes.

When the cake is done, remove from the oven, undo the springform clip, remove the side ring and gently slide the cake from the metal base onto a wire rack.

Serve warm, with icing sugar dusted over the top.

MY GODMOTHER ROSALIND'S POACHED PEACHES IN WHITE WINE SYRUP

Unless it's the height of summer, peaches invariably disappoint. They go from rock hard to fluff in seconds, missing that perfect moment where one bite sends juice cascading down your chin.

Poaching indifferent peaches is an excellent way to turn them into something quite lovely. Peeling them is a little bit of a faff, but it's worth the effort, especially as, if you choose peaches with a dark-pink skin, the colour imprints itself onto the flesh beneath. My beloved godmother taught me how to peel and poach a peach one summer holiday when I was about twelve: it's actually very easy to do. Don't bother trying this with imported peaches in the dead of winter – it's almost impossible to shuck the skins off the bullet-like fruit.

If you like, go the whole hog and make peach melba – as my Norfolk granny would do if we begged, with a ball of vanilla ice cream perched over each half and raspberry purée poured over it all.

SERVES 4
375ml water
1 vanilla pod (optional)
500ml white wine
50g caster sugar
4 peaches
thick cream, to serve

METHOD
Place the water, vanilla pod, if using, wine and sugar in a heavy-bottomed saucepan and bring to the boil. Place the peaches in the liquid, reduce the heat to a gentle simmer and poach for 20 minutes, making sure that you move the peaches around occasionally so that they cook evenly.

Remove them from the pan with a slotted spoon and allow to cool. Peel the skin off very carefully.

Put the pan back on the heat and boil the liquid until it has reduced by about half and you have a thick syrup. Allow to cool slightly.

I serve these in a little glass bowl, with a spoonful of syrup poured over and thick cream in a jug nearby.

HOT-CROSS-BUN BREAD-AND-BUTTER PUDDING

One summer in France, I found a big bag of hard, stale pains au chocolat hiding in a kitchen cupboard in our holiday home. I cannot abide waste so I cut them into fat slices, popped them in a dish with some large chunks of dark chocolate that I happened to have lurking in my handbag for emergencies, and poured over a rough-and-ready custard: a mixture of eggs, sugar, cream and milk. Basically, bread-and-butter pudding, but with French pastries. It was one of the most delicious things I've ever eaten.

I traditionally hate bread-and-butter pudding. Loathe it. The difference here lies in the quality of the ingredients and because you aren't dealing with thin, mushy slices of bread, there's more crunch and texture going on.

Anyway, the following Easter I found myself with a six-pack of stale hot cross buns. (It's quite extraordinary that this could happen in my household, where the usual manner of hot-cross-bun consumption is inhalation.) So I thought I would give them the baked custard treatment, too. And I found that it was good. Very good. So if you have some leftover buns after the Easter festivities, then this is what I suggest you do with them.

The glorious thing about this recipe is that when you remove the dish from the oven, the hot cross buns have miraculously risen like Yorkshire puddings. It really looks spectacular, so I do recommend not putting this in the oven until 30 minutes before you intend to eat it, as you'll want to serve it all puffed up with pride.

Because this is a quick recipe, I didn't make a proper, thickened custard first as the mixture thickens in the oven. Neither did I infuse my cream and milk with a vanilla pod, so I added vanilla paste instead, which has the little, dark seeds you would get from splitting and scraping out the pod. At the last minute, I decided to add a generous slosh of orange essence to the custard, which gave it a heavenly perfume.

SERVES 6

6 hot cross buns
30g butter
handful chocolate chips (optional)
4 eggs
350ml single cream
350ml whole milk
30g sugar, plus extra for sprinkling
1 tsp ground cinnamon
1 tsp vanilla extract, or 1 heaped tsp vanilla paste
orange zest, orange essence, candied peel, sultanas, raisins, currants (use just one, or a combination of these, as you prefer; all are optional)

METHOD
Preheat the oven to 180°C/350°F/gas mark 4.

Slice open the hot cross buns and liberally butter each side. Place the halves in a dish just big enough for them all. (If adding chocolate, tuck in some chips around the buns.)

In a bowl mix together the eggs, single cream and milk. Whisk in the sugar and cinnamon.

Then add the vanilla. If using orange zest, orange essence, candied peel, sultanas, raisins and/or currants, tip them in now.

Pour over your buns and sprinkle over a little extra sugar for crunch. You'll need to squish down your buns into the liquid, to help them soak it all up. Otherwise, they float.

Bake for approximately 30 minutes.

Try not to open the oven door until you think they are ready, as you run the risk of your lovely, puffy pudding collapsing.

Flower Markets

I like little more than a posy of blowsy roses cut from the garden: they can transform a table – see page 155 for some of my tips. If I don't have access to a garden, then a flower market is a truly wonderful thing.

London

Many people don't realise that members of the public can buy from New Covent Garden. You'll be buying wraps – a group of bunches at a time, but often at an advantageous price. (That's the pay-off for getting there at 5am.) Open Monday to Saturday, midnight to 10am (core trading hours are from 4am); www.newcoventgardenmarket.com

New York

I head either to Chelsea – the Flower District is around 28th Street between 6th and 7th Avenues – or pick up $10 bunches of roses from the bodegas on every street corner.

Amsterdam

A floating flower market? There's only one in the world: the Bloemenmarkt on Amsterdam's Singel canal. Open Monday to Saturday, 9am to 5.30pm; Sunday 11am to 5.30pm; www.iamsterdam.com

BAKED APPLES WITH CINNAMON AND DRIED FRUIT

A baked apple's appeal is all in the light-as-a-cloud fluff of the flesh, mixed with the plump dried fruit and the caramelisation of the butter and sugar. Rich, sticky, sinful – and perfect with cold double cream.

I often see recipes suggesting that the apples will cook in 25 minutes but this is a bit optimistic, and if they are those lovely, large ones you may want to allow at least 40 minutes. The best thing is that they are terribly forgiving and, even if you forget about them, there's nothing not to like about handing out bowls of apple fluff (where they have burst out of their skins.)

The **essential** thing is to make sure you score around their middles with a sharp knife, cutting a good centimetre in, as this will stop the apples exploding in the oven. Take it from me: there is nothing enjoyable about scrubbing carbonised apple off the back of the oven.

SERVES 4

4 fat Bramley cooking apples
60g light muscovado sugar
100g dried fruit (any combination of sultanas, raisins, currants, candied peel, chopped apricots)
80g butter, softened
½ tsp ground cinnamon

METHOD

Preheat the oven to 180°C/350°F/gas mark 4.

Wash, core and then score the apples all the way around their middles, 1cm deep.

Muscovado can get terribly lumpy, so you'll need to push it through a sieve with your fingers, into a bowl. Add the dried fruit and the butter. Using your hands, mash together the ingredients to form a paste. Stuff this into the apple cores, turning the apples over to check it has gone all the way to the bottom.

Place in an ovenproof dish and cook for 25–40 minutes, depending on the size of the apples.

> **SECRET**
> Buy an apple corer for a few pounds. Your fingers will thank you.

EVE'S PUDDING, THREE WAYS

Eve's pudding – one of my favourite, classic English puddings – is something I first ate at school, where we were often served it doused in custard. Now I prefer it with cream or ice cream, but it's just as good on its own.

Traditionally made from Bramley apples, a tart variety of English apple also known as cookers, it's essentially a hot sponge cake with soft, slightly tart apples, which stew underneath as the sponge bakes above.

Lots of fruits work in this. I like adding a quince to the apples in the autumn; raspberries or blackberries would also be a good addition to apples or peaches.

It can be made in pretty much any kind of ovenproof dish, as it is not turned out at the end of cooking. Don't forget to sprinkle the sugar over the cake mixture before you put it in the oven, to get a lovely, crunchy top.

SERVES 4–6

110g butter, softened, plus
**   extra for greasing (do NOT use**
**   margarine or the baking gods**
**   will strike you down)**
3 Bramley cooking apples
110g sugar, plus extra
**   for sprinkling**
2 large eggs
110g self-raising flour
splash of vanilla extract

METHOD

Preheat the oven to 180°C/350°F/gas mark 4 and generously grease a medium, ovenproof dish.

Peel and core the apples. Chop them into large bite-size pieces and put them in the ovenproof dish.

Cream together the butter and the sugar with a wooden spoon or in a food processor. I favour the latter. When you're done, it should be light and fluffy.

Add 1 egg, beat. Add a large scoop of flour, beat. Add the second egg, beat. Add the rest of the flour. Add the vanilla, beat. It's really that simple.

Spread the mixture over the top of the fruit. Sprinkle with extra sugar and bake for about 25–30 minutes.

WITH NECTARINES AND BLUEBERRIES

I first made this version of Eve's Pudding for a group of friends when we wanted a very quick, comforting, warm pudding after a day of surfing in the cold Cornish sea. It was the end of August and this felt like the perfect cake to straddle the dog days of summer and the beginning of autumn: it has both tart and sweet summer fruits, against the comfort of hot sponge. You need two nectarines, chopped and pitted and one cup of blueberries (or enough to fill your chosen oven dish). You could sub peaches for the nectarines, but I prefer nectarines as they keep their shape a bit better. (Peaches do tend to mush quite easily.) Follow the instructions for the apple recipe, opposite, replacing the apples with the nectarines and blueberries.

WITH APRICOTS AND ALMONDS

You will need eight to ten apricots, halved and pitted (or enough to fill your chosen oven dish). Follow the instructions for the apple recipe, opposite, replacing the apples with the apricots and sprinkling with 1 dsp sugar, and replacing 40g of the flour with ground almonds.

CAKES AND AFTERNOON TEA

Whether I am sitting in a grand-luxe hotel eyeing a stand of teeny-tiny sandwiches, or lolling in front of a fire in the winter at home eating crumpets dripping with butter, afternoon tea will never, ever lose its appeal for me.

Sadly, now that I am older, eating afternoon tea means skipping lunch – and possibly supper, as well. That's because a traditional afternoon tea includes scones, sandwiches, cakes and biscuits. In this chapter I have focused on the cake-and-biscuit side of things – I don't think anyone needs a recipe for cucumber or smoked salmon sandwiches. Just remember to season properly and to cut the crusts off.

The cakes here are split between what I think of pudding cakes (ones that could be served warm after the main course, with cream or ice cream) and cold, showstopper cakes (the ones that will impress everyone, but are surprisingly uncomplicated to make).

One thing I have learnt from my blog is that although lots of people are horrified at the idea of making a cake from scratch, once they make their first one, they're astonished that it could be so simple. (Cakes were the first thing that I mastered in the kitchen as a little girl.)

I think it's handy to have one cake recipe and one biscuit recipe in your repertoire that you can make and adapt at will. The important thing to remember is that baking is a science: you need accurate scales and don't be tempted to try to freestyle the proportions of butter, sugar and flour.

However, if you like Herman's Rhubarb Cake (see page 160), there's no reason why you couldn't try it with plums; or if you can't find Ferrero Rochers for the Ambassador's Cake (see page 149), use smashed-up chocolate wafers instead. The key is to play with the flavourings, not the building blocks.

The single most important thing to learn in cake-making is not to overmix the batter once the flour has been added – this will overstretch the gluten in the flour and give you a leaden, heavy cake.

TRIPLE-LAYER LEMON CAKE
WITH FRESH BLACKBERRY JAM
AND BLACKBERRY SWISS MERINGUE
BUTTERCREAM

This cake is my show-stopper: it has never, ever failed me and never, ever fails to impress. I think everyone needs one cake that they can wheel out for special occasions and, once you have mastered this, you will always have the perfect cake for any occasion in your repertoire.

It's based on a classic Victoria sponge, which holds up perfectly. Because I am not great at splitting cakes with a knife, I bake three layers to sandwich together. The icing is a light and fluffy, delectably smooth, meringue-based dream.

SERVES 12 GENEROUSLY

1 quantity Fresh Blackberry Jam (page 146)
1 quantity Swiss Meringue Buttercream (page 146), flavoured with juice from the Fresh Blackberry Jam
small punnet blackberries, for decoration

For the Victoria sponge
375g self-raising flour
2 tsp baking powder
375g butter, softened
375g caster sugar
grated zest of 2 lemons
6 eggs
3 x 20cm round cake tins, greased and lined with baking paper

SECRET
It's best to buy springform, loose-bottomed cake tins, as there is less chance of the cake mixture sticking to the tin.

METHOD

For the Victoria sponge, preheat the oven to 180°C/350°F/gas mark 4. Sift the flour and baking powder into a bowl.

Put the butter, sugar and lemon zest into a large mixing bowl and beat with a wooden spoon or a hand-held electric whisk until light and fluffy. Add 1 egg at a time, along with a spoonful of flour, to the butter mixture to prevent the mixture curdling. Add the rest of the flour, a big spoonful at a time, being careful to stop beating the moment the flour is incorporated. (Overbeating leads to a heavier cake.) Divide the mixture equally between the cake tins and bake for 25–30 minutes. Allow the cakes to cool for 10 minutes before turning them out of the tins and allowing them to cool completely on wire racks.

Spoon half the Fresh Blackberry Jam over one layer of cake to form the bottom, being careful to gently squish the blackberries into the cake. (This allows for a pretty effect when the cake is cut.) Repeat on a second layer. Take the Swiss Meringue Buttercream, put a dollop on the bottom layer, and carefully spread out from the middle with a knife over all the jam. Resist the temptation to use too much, as it will just squirt out of the sides. Carefully place the next jam-covered layer of cake on top, and repeat the buttercream process.

Then add the final layer of cake. Smooth the remainder of the buttercream on the top and around the sides, paying special attention to the gaps between the layers, which you should fill in with extra icing. Decorate with blackberries.

SWISS MERINGUE BUTTERCREAM

SMB is lighter than normal buttercream and is consequently much easier to spread. It calls for a weight of egg whites, as egg sizes are imprecise. I've had great success using cartons of pasteurised egg whites, but if you use whole eggs remember that yolks freeze (don't forget to write the quantity on the container).

You will need both an hand-held electric whisk and a stand mixer to make this icing (unless you have wrists of steel) along with a cooking thermometer. I strongly suggest investing in a digital one.

MAKES ENOUGH FOR A TRIPLE-LAYER CAKE
340g egg whites (approx. 8 eggs)
625g caster sugar
625g soft butter, cut into pieces
3 tsp vanilla extract
3 tbsp juice from Fresh Blackberry Jam (see right), to colour the buttercream

METHOD
Place a large saucepan over a medium heat and quarter-fill with water, placing the metal bowl from a stand mixer over the water in the pan. Alternatively, use a heatproof bowl. Pour in the egg whites and sugar and start beating together with a hand-held electric whisk. Place the thermometer in the mixture and beat constantly until it reaches 60°C. This will take at least 5 minutes. Now remove the metal bowl from the pan to the stand mixer and beat on high until it is glossy and peaked, and both the meringue and bowl are completely cool (about 10 minutes).

Swap the beater attachment for the whisk and start adding the butter pieces with the motor still running. When it is all incorporated, add the vanilla and juice and beat for 5 minutes.

Very occasionally, SMB curdles in the mixer. Don't cry: there is a simple rescue. Remove 4 heaped spoonfuls and microwave on high for 15 seconds. Place back in the mixer bowl and beat again, gradually increasing the speed, until smooth again.

FRESH BLACKBERRY JAM

I love a fruit layer in sponge cakes, but I am not so keen on using jam: I find it too sweet, too heavy and too sticky. This recipe came about when I was trying to find an alternative to jam that was thicker than a compote, so it wouldn't run off the cake, but not so dense that it wouldn't spread. (A recipe in US *Country Living* magazine was the starting point for this idea.) It's essentially soft fruit, made to give up its juices by the addition of a little sugar and heat, and thickened with cornflour.

MAKES APPROX. 1 JAM JAR
375g fresh or frozen blackberries
1 tbsp crème de mûre, or any fruit liqueur (optional)
70g sugar
1 tbsp fresh lemon juice
1 tbsp cornflour
2 tbsp water

METHOD
Place the blackberries, fruit liqueur, if using, sugar and lemon juice in a saucepan and heat very gently until the blackberries begin to soften and give up their juice.

Using a slotted spoon, remove the blackberries to a bowl and squash them gently with the back of a spoon. Set a sieve over the saucepan and strain the juice back in. Set the strained berries aside.

Sift the cornflour into a small bowl (this is important or you will get lumps), and add the 2 tbsp water, stirring briskly with a teaspoon or mini whisk to ensure the water and flour are wholly combined.

Put the mixture into the berry juice, stir and bring to the boil. Lower the heat and simmer until the mixture is thick and jam-like. Pour in the reserved blackberries, stir and then tip the jam into a clean bowl to cool.

If using in a cake, make sure it is completely cool first. It will keep for 2–3 days in the fridge.

VANILLA FAIRY CAKES
WITH FRESH RASPBERRIES
AND RASPBERRY FROSTING

I think food that has a surprise inside is always beguiling, and these pale pink, raspberry-flecked, iced fairy cakes look like the simplest cakes on the tea table. But when you cut them in half, there's a fresh raspberry lurking in the middle, giving a lovely sharp contrast to the creamy icing.

I use buttermilk in these cupcakes as I like the tang and lightness that it gives to the sponge. If you don't have buttermilk, simply add lemon juice to milk. The usual proportion is 250ml milk to 15ml lemon juice. This gives you a good excuse to make my Buttermilk Pancakes (see page 12) with the leftovers.

MAKES 12
110g butter, softened
110g golden caster sugar
2 eggs
1 tsp vanilla extract
80g self-raising flour, sifted
30g ground almonds
24 raspberries

For the frosting
125g butter, softened
250g icing sugar
1 tbsp milk
2 tsp raspberry jam
8 raspberries
12-hole cupcake tin, lined with paper cupcake cases

METHOD
Preheat the oven to 180°C/350°F/gas mark 4.

Cream together the butter and the sugar with a wooden spoon or a hand-held electric whisk until light and fluffy. Beat in the eggs and vanilla.

Mix together the flour and ground almonds in a separate bowl. Now fold into the egg mixture.

Divide the mixture between the 12 cupcake cases (I use a small ice-cream scoop). Bake for 15–20 minutes, or until risen and golden.

Tip the baked fairy cakes out of the tin and allow to cool completely on a wire rack.

For the frosting, put the butter in a large mixing bowl. Sift the icing sugar into the bowl, a little at a time, beating it into the butter until smooth. Then, beat in the milk and raspberry jam. Squash the raspberries with the back of a fork, then beat into the frosting until evenly incorporated.

Using a small, very sharp knife, scoop out a raspberry-sized hole in the top of each fairy cake. Insert a raspberry.

The frosting can either be piped on in swirls, using a piping bag, or smoothed on with the flat of a knife. Top with another raspberry.

THE AMBASSADOR'S CAKE
(OR MILK CHOCOLATE LAYER CAKE)

I like to think this is what the Ambassador's chef makes with all the Ferrero Rochers left over from his receptions. This is my slightly more adult riff on the first chocolate cake I can remember eating, which was billed as a milk chocolate cake because it used drinking chocolate in the sponge as opposed to proper, grown-up chocolate. This makes it great for children, as it's not at all rich but, because it has a proper chocolate icing, it still delivers that delicious theobromine hit. The evaporated milk is a clever touch because it makes for a deliciously light and moist crumb.

SERVES 10–12

375g self-raising flour
4 tbsp drinking chocolate
6 tbsp cocoa powder
450g caster sugar
½ tsp salt
200g butter
4 eggs
5 tbsp evaporated milk
5 tbsp water
2 tsp vanilla extract

For the chocolate fudge icing
16 chocolate wafer truffles
   (I use Ferrero Rocher)
175g butter
8 tbsp cocoa powder, sifted
8 tbsp evaporated milk
2 tsp vanilla extract
600g icing sugar
two deep, 20cm round
   springform or loose-bottomed
   cake tins, greased

METHOD

Preheat the oven to 180°C/350°F/gas mark 4.

Tip the dry ingredients and the butter in a food processor and whizz together. You can make this in a stand mixer, but the processor makes for a smoother batter.

Mix together all the liquid ingredients, then add to the processor. Whizz together until the mixture is well combined, but be careful not to overbeat as this will result in a heavy cake. Divide the mixture between the greased cake tins, smoothing off the top.

Bake for about 45–50 minutes. The cake should be springy when pressed with a finger, and a skewer inserted in the middle will come out clean. Turn out carefully onto a wire rack and allow to cool for at least 1 hour before icing.

For the chocolate fudge icing, smash up 10 of the chocolate wafer truffles and set aside. Put the butter in a saucepan over a very low heat and tip in the cocoa. Whisk together as the butter melts.

Combine the evaporated milk and vanilla in either a stand mixer or a large mixing bowl. Remove the cocoa and butter from the heat, add to the milk mixture and beat well. Sift in the icing sugar gradually (do not skip the sifting or you will end up with lumpy icing) and beat very well in either the mixer or with a wooden spoon until smooth. Do not add all the sugar at once as the icing becomes impossible to stir. Once mixed, use immediately as it hardens quickly.

In a small bowl place 2 generous tablespoons of the icing and mix with the smashed chocolates. Dollop the mixture on top of one cake layer, spread it out evenly and then sandwich with the second cake layer. Ice the top with the remaining icing, smoothing with a spatula down towards the side. Then ice the sides. Dipping the spatula in water will help smooth the icing. Decorate the top immediately with the 6 remaining chocolate wafer truffles.

SECRET
If you have stupendous self-control, this cake not only keeps very well, but it travels perfectly, as the fudge icing is quite firm.

BROWNIES

If I had to name a signature bake, this would be it. I've made these brownies in kitchens all over the world, for friends and for enemies. There are very few people who can resist the lure of these squidgy, intensely chocolatey squares.

Best of all, they take less than ten minutes to prepare, so are a great last-minute present or treat. I sometimes serve them warm as pudding with chocolate sauce and ice cream and, chopped up small, they are a vital part of my Hot Brownie Sundae (see page 186) and Individual Chocolate Trifles (see page 129).

I like to use golden (caster or granulated) sugar in this recipe, as it gives a more caramelly taste, but it's not essential. Note that cake-release spray, available online and in some supermarkets and cookshops, is a godsend for making brownies as the nuts can often stick to the sides of the cake tin. Otherwise make sure you thoroughly line the tin with greaseproof paper or a silicone baking sheet.

MAKES 8–10
175g chocolate (I like 70% cocoa solids)
175g butter
3 eggs
200g golden caster or granulated sugar
1 tbsp vanilla extract
150g walnuts, chopped
110g plain flour, sifted
pinch of salt
20 x 20cm baking tin, greased or lined with greaseproof paper

METHOD
Melt the chocolate and the butter together in a heavy saucepan over a very low heat. If you are nervous about the chocolate burning (or if the pan is lightweight), simply pour boiling water into the pan and place a heatproof bowl – such as Pyrex – over the water so that it fits without touching the water. Put the chocolate and butter in the bowl and allow to melt.

When the chocolate and butter have melted, remove from the heat and allow to cool for about 5–10 minutes. This is so the eggs do not scramble when they are added to the hot mixture.

Beat together the eggs, sugar and vanilla. Add the melted chocolate and butter mixture to the eggs and beat. Then tip in the walnuts, flour and salt. Make sure everything is thoroughly mixed together, as the flour has a habit of forming bubbles.

Pour the mixture into the prepared tin and bake for approximately 25 minutes. They should still be squidgy in the middle. Remove the tin from the oven and allow the brownies to cool in the tin.

Tip the brownies out onto a board and cut into 8–10 portions.

SECRET
If you want a truly luxurious treat, plop a teaspoon of hazelnut chocolate spread at regular intervals into the batter once it is in the tin.

PLUM AND ALMOND LITTLE CAKES

These are made in a traditional muffin tin without paper muffin cases. This results in lovely miniature cakes, as opposed to cupcake shapes. I recommend a silicone muffin tin here, but if you don't have one, use either butter or cake release spray to thoroughly grease the holes of the tin.

MAKES 12
150g butter
100g caster or granulated
  sugar, plus extra for
  sprinkling
50g light muscovado sugar
3 eggs
1 tsp almond extract
100g self-raising flour, sifted
1 tsp baking powder
50g ground almonds
100g plums, pitted and
  chopped
12-hole muffin tin (silicone is
  best here)

METHOD
Preheat the oven to 180°C/350°F/gas mark 4.

Cream together the butter and both sugars with a wooden spoon or a hand-held electric whisk until light and fluffy. Then add the eggs and almond extract, followed by the flour, baking powder and ground almonds.

Then, using a metal spoon, fold in the chopped plums.

Divide the mixture between the 12 holes of the muffin tin (I use a small ice-cream scoop).

Sprinkle a little granulated sugar over the top of each cake. Bake for 15–20 minutes, or until risen and golden.

Tip the little cakes out of the tin and allow to cool on a wire rack.

CHOCOLATE CHUNK COOKIES

I am obsessed with baking the perfect chocolate chip cookie. This is partly because, historically, biscuits have not been an area where I shine, but also because I want a go-to biscuit recipe that I can knock up in under half an hour, with no dough resting overnight in the fridge, or special measures required.

I like to use bars of 70-per-cent chocolate as opposed to chocolate chips. I chop them up myself with a large knife, which gives lots of tiny scrapings and creates an attractively striated effect when baked. Because I use chocolate with a higher proportion of cocoa solids, the cookies are slightly less sweet than you may expect. What's more, they are not delicate, friable biscuits, or those bendy, almost-raw-in-the-middle cookies of shopping malls; nor are they parsimonious with the chocolate. What they are is a beguiling combination of crisp, thick and chewy.

MAKES APPROX. 20

250g dark chocolate
175g golden caster sugar
50g light muscovado sugar
150g butter, softened
2 tsp vanilla extract
1 whole egg, fridge-cold
1 egg yolk, fridge-cold
300g plain flour
½ tsp baking powder
3 baking trays lined with greaseproof paper or silicone baking sheets, or just greased

METHOD
Preheat the oven to 180°C/350°F/gas mark 4.

Break up the chocolate into pieces, then take a large knife and, using a rocking action, chop into little chunks. (To do this, place one hand flat on top of the knife tip and one curved around the handle as normal.) Make sure you reserve all the little scrapings.

Pour both sugars into a mixing bowl. Mash out any lumps in the muscovado sugar with a fork. Add the butter, and cream together with a wooden spoon or a hand-held electric whisk until light and fluffy. Add the vanilla and eggs and beat again thoroughly.

Sift in the flour and baking powder: it will seem like a lot, but don't worry. Beat everything together but be very careful not to overmix. Carefully stir in the chocolate by hand, making sure it is evenly distributed through the dough.

This is a nice, thick dough. Use either a small ice-cream scoop for super-even cookies, or just scoop up small balls with a spoon.

Gently flatten them out on the baking trays, so they look like hockey pucks and lay them out in 2 long rows per tray leaving plenty of room for the cookies to spread out. Six should fit on a standard, rectangular tray.

Bake for about 15 minutes. They will go quite golden because of the sugars and will be a little floppy in the middle from the melted chocolate, so leave them to cool on the baking trays for 5 minutes, then carefully lift with a spatula to a wire rack to cool.

POMEGRANATE MOLASSES SPICE COOKIES

Molasses cookies (made from molasses, or treacle) are a classic American recipe, and I developed mine after tasting a memorable version on a road trip through central California.

As for pomegranate molasses, it's extraordinary how many people now have a bottle of this lurking in a kitchen cupboard, which comes out maybe once a month. I like it drizzled over halloumi for a quick lunch and it's an integral part of my roast cauliflower salad, but the huge bottle is still sitting there half full and sticky. When I came back to England I wondered what would happen if I added pomegranate molasses to my standard molasses cookie recipe. It was a great success: the pomegranate cuts the sweetness and enhances the spice.

I use bicarbonate of soda rather than baking powder in this recipe, as molasses is a reagent for bicarb (it gets rid of the bitter taste), but it does mean you need to bake the cookie dough immediately, as the reaction starts in the mixing bowl.

MAKES APPROX. 15
120g butter, softened
70g molasses (the sugar, not the pomegranate syrup)
70g light muscovado sugar
60g caster sugar
1 egg
50g pomegranate molasses
275g plain flour
2 tsp bicarbonate of soda
1 tsp ground cinnamon
2 tsp ground allspice
1½ tsp ground ginger
2–3 baking trays lined with greaseproof paper or silicone baking sheets, or just greased

METHOD
Preheat the oven to 180°C/350°F/gas mark 4.

Cream together the butter, molasses and both sugars. (This is best done in a food processor, as the sugars are very dense.)

Beat the egg and pomegranate molasses together and add to the butter and sugar mixture, mixing in well.

Sift together the flour, bicarbonate of soda and spices and add to the bowl, being careful not to overmix.

Use your hands to create balls of dough about the size of a chocolate truffle and place them on the baking trays but do not press each ball down. Leave plenty of room for them to spread out, and count on fitting about 6 on a standard baking tray.

Bake for 20–25 minutes. The cookies are done when they are crisp around the edges but still slightly soft in the middle – they will harden as they cool, so be careful lifting them off the baking tray.

NUTTY CHOCOLATE PALMIERS

I take a great deal of pleasure in baking boxes and boxes full of cakes, muffins, biscuits, fudge and other sweets to deliver as thank-you Christmas presents. Amongst them are always these palmiers, which are a doddle to make and are fun to do with children too, as all they involve is a bit of pastry rolling and some Nutella spreading.

They are especially good eaten warm (not piping hot) from the oven, as the flaky pastry showers over your frock as you bite into them and the warm Nutella and butter drips down your wrist.

MAKES APPROX. 26
flour, for dusting
375g ready-made puff pastry (pre-rolled, preferably)
140g hazelnut chocolate spread (Nutella can't be beaten)
60g chopped, toasted nuts (hazelnuts, pecans, almonds, peanuts are all good)
1 egg, lightly beaten
granulated sugar, for sprinkling
1–2 baking trays lined with greaseproof paper or silicone baking sheets, or just greased

METHOD
Preheat the oven to 180°C/350°F/gas mark 4.

Sprinkle some flour over a work surface and remove the pastry from its wrapping. If using pre-rolled, roll it out once with a rolling pin, in one direction. (It doesn't rise properly if you mess it about too much.) If rolling out a square of pastry, roll it to a thickness of about 0.5cm.

Scoop the hazelnut chocolate spread out into a bowl and heat it gently in a bain-marie, or a bowl set over a pan of simmering water, until it loosens. Be careful not to overheat, as it can separate. (The packaging specifically warns against microwaving.)

Take a knife, dip it in the bain-marie or saucepan of boiling water and then dip it into the spread. Spread the chocolate all over the flattened pastry, then scatter the chopped nuts all over the top. Now roll up each long side towards the middle until they meet.

Using a very sharp knife, cut the roll into 1.5cm slices. Use the flat of a cook's knife to gently squash them flat.

Set the palmiers out on the baking trays, giving them enough room to spread during cooking – you should be able to fit 4 across. Brush each palmier with beaten egg and sprinkle sugar over the top.

Bake for 25 minutes for the palmiers to turn a light, golden brown, but check at 20. Using a spatula (the chocolate spread gets boiling hot so use fingers at your peril), lift them off the baking trays onto a wire rack to cool down.

If one palmier needs to be tested for deliciousness immediately, do watch out for the very hot chocolate spread. And do wait until the palmiers are completely cool before putting them into a tin, otherwise they will go soggy.

FLOWERS FOR THE KITCHEN TABLE

It's a wonderful indulgence to have flowers on my kitchen table when friends come round to eat. Of course, I don't have time to create lavish arrangements but a few simple tricks can transform a bunch or two of inexpensive flowers into something rather impressive.

I always keep odd-shaped glass jars once they are empty, along with medicine bottles, small jam jars and the glasses from scented candles, as they all make great vases.

The quickest trick is to tie a piece of string loosely under the heads of a single bunch of roses and chop off the stems quite short, to the height of the (small-ish) vase you wish to place them in. This will give a wonderful massed effect. Do make sure the vase you choose isn't too tall – about 15cm is perfect.

After the liquid has evaporated from the little square or round glass vessels that are used as scent diffusers, I wash the bottles and use a cluster of three or five (always odd numbers) as tiny vases, clustered together. A single rose; a stalk of veronica; maybe a piece of eucalyptus and a piece of scented stock; or an open ranunculus or anemone: a stem in each vase, cut at different heights, always looks charming.

If you use jam jars as vases, a handy trick is to think in thirds: the height of the flowers sticking out of the top of the jam jar should be twice the height of the jar.

ICE-CREAM BIRTHDAY CAKE

My sister Holly's birthday falls in the middle of August and, for all the years of our childhood, our mother made an ice-cream birthday cake adapted from a Delia Smith recipe, for her party. (That's Holly and our mother Victoria in the photo to the right with this very cake.)

It's a super-light whisked sponge cake, split and layered with vanilla ice cream. The sides are held together with sugary sponge fingers painted with apricot jam to stick them onto the sides of the cake; semi-set jelly is poured over the top, and the whole lot bunged in the freezer to settle and firm up. (Believe me, frozen jelly is delicious.)

Of course we had our own family twist on it. One year we had no strawberry jelly for the frozen top, so my mother used lime green. Although we all preferred pink jelly, the radioactive look became a family tradition.

SERVES 10–12

For the whisked sponge cake
200g self-raising flour, plus extra for dusting
8 eggs
200g caster sugar
1 tsp baking powder

For the filling and topping
1.5 litres vanilla ice cream
1 packet pink jelly
2 tbsp seedless jam (apricot is good)
1½ packets (approx. 30) sponge fingers or Boudoir biscuits
two deep, 20cm round springform or loose-bottomed cake tins, greased
one very deep, 20cm round cake tin (preferably springform), sides and base lined with greaseproof paper
ribbon, to tie around the middle

METHOD

For the whisked sponge cake, preheat the oven to 180°C/350°F/gas mark 4. Tip a teaspoon of extra flour into each of the two greased cake tins and shake them about to coat the insides evenly in flour.

Put the eggs and sugar into a large mixing bowl and whisk with a hand-held electric whisk until very thick and pale. When you can lift the beaters and leave a thin ribbon train sitting on the mixture, it is ready. This will take 5–10 minutes depending on the freshness of the eggs.

Sift together the flour and baking powder, then carefully fold them into the egg batter using a metal spoon. Be careful not to overmix it, as you need as much air as possible to allow the cake to rise.

Divide the mixture equally between the prepared cake tins and bake for 25–30 minutes. A skewer inserted in the middle should come out clean. Run a knife around the insides of the tins and turn out on to a wire rack. The cakes must be completely cooled before you ice them – this takes around 1 hour.

Take the ice cream out of the freezer about 20 minutes before you need it, to allow to soften slightly.

When the cakes are cool, check them to see how level they are and, if necessary, use a serrated knife carefully to flatten the tops. Choose the neater for the top layer. Carefully slice each cake layer in half horizontally to give 4 layers of sponge in total.

Now fit one cake layer into the base of the deep, lined cake tin and spoon one-third of the ice cream over it, spreading it out evenly. Place another sponge layer on top of the ice cream, followed by a another third of ice cream, the third layer of sponge and the final third of ice cream. Top with the fourth sponge layer.

Tightly cover the top of the cake tin with foil and freeze the cake overnight. (You can leave it for several days in the freezer.)

The morning of the day on which you wish to serve the cake, make the jelly in a shallow bowl, dissolving it in 275ml **only** of hot water. (Ignore the packet instructions.)

Remove the cake from the freezer, take off the foil, and slowly and carefully spoon the jelly all over the surface, where it will start to set almost immediately because of the ice-cold cake. Don't worry if any jelly makes a break for freedom; it won't show once the sides of the cake are covered with biscuits.

Cover the cake with the foil once again and return to the freezer for at least 1 hour. (You can store it in this state for up to a month although my patience has never lasted this long.)

Take the cake out of the freezer at least 1 hour before serving. Meanwhile, gently warm the jam in a small saucepan.

Hold a hot, damp dishcloth round the tin for a few seconds, then ease the cake gently upwards from the tin ring by pushing on the loose base. Slide a spatula underneath between the cake and the tin base, and transfer the cake onto a plate.

Now spread the plain sides of the sponge fingers with the warm jam and position them vertically all around the side of the cake.

Use the ribbon to hold the sponge fingers in place as you position them. (You may find a few pins helpful here.) Keep in the fridge until needed.

Wonderful Places to Drink Tea and Eat Cake

NEW YORK: Cha-An

A few blocks from my first apartment in the East Village, Cha-An does an afternoon tea that's both delicious and inexpensive. It's also unexpected: this is a Japanese tea house and their decidedly untraditional take includes matcha shortbread, Earl-Grey scones and ten types of green tea.

230 East 9th Street, New York, NY 10003; www.chaanteahouse.com

LONDON: The Modern Pantry

Any of the grand London hotels like The Connaught, Claridge's or The Dorchester will serve an immaculate afternoon tea, with much white-glove ritual, but I also like the low-key, traditional charm of The Goring (hard by Buckingham Palace), or the leftfield take of The Modern Pantry in Clerkenwell, where the chocolate-mousse cake is spiked with chilli and liquorice, and the dacquoise is made with green tea and toasted, black sesame seeds.

The Modern Pantry, 47–48 St John's Square, London EC1V 4JJ; www.themodernpantry.co.uk

BERLIN: Barcomi's Deli and Café

I first visited Barcomi's – hidden off a charming, secret courtyard – when I was directed there by a flurry of recommendations on Twitter. There is a huge display case full of the most delicious cakes: those showing restraint can order a single slice. Others (ahem, myself) can order a tasting plate with a slice from four different cakes. (The cheesecake is as if made by angels.)

Sophienstraße 21, 10178 Berlin; www.barcomis.de

SAN FRANCISCO: Japanese Tea Garden

This beautiful tea garden, inside San Francisco's Golden Gate Park, has long been one of my favourite places to sit and serenely contemplate my navel. When I am not feeling so introspective, I eat dorayaki (pancakes filled with red bean paste) and watch the Japanese tea ceremony demonstrations inside the authentic tea house. The best time to visit is in March and April when the cherry blossoms bloom.

75 Hagiwara Tea Garden Drive, San Francisco CA 94118; www.japaneseteagardensf.com

HERMAN'S RHUBARB CAKE WITH CRUMBLE TOPPING

I spend a few weeks each summer at the French home of Herman, the father of a dear old school friend. It's a farmhouse set in the middle of fields, and the shops are an energetic bike ride away. I bake endless cakes for the legions of family who appear without warning, so imagine my joy on discovering copious rhubarb patches all around the house. I take enormous pleasure in wandering out into the intense August heat, armed with an ancient wooden-handled knife, and kneeling in the grass to cut the rhubarb stalks. I trim them then and there, tossing the umbrella leaves into the compost bin under the kitchen window.

This is the perfect cake for feeding a big, hungry family; it serves ten as a warm pudding cake, with custard. It always goes down like a house on fire: the French cake-eating record is three slices down one gullet at one sitting.

It's also quick to make: with a food processor it can be done in 15 minutes. It does take a while to cook, though: depending on your oven, you need to allow up to an hour and a half for it to cook through.

For this cake, it's better to go for a wide tin than a deeper one if you have a choice, as it will take far too long to cook otherwise, and you risk a dark brown outside and molten middle. (I once made this cake in a pan so wide that my batter was only 5cm high, and it still tasted delicious.)

SERVES 10
400g butter, softened
400g caster sugar
6 eggs
400g self-raising flour
500g rhubarb stalks, chopped into 2cm pieces and tossed with 1 tbsp sugar

For the crumble topping
150g fridge-cold butter, cut into cubes
150g plain flour
30g caster sugar
23cm springform or loose-bottomed cake tin, greased, and base and sides lined with greaseproof paper

METHOD
Preheat the oven to 180°C/350°F/gas mark 4.

In a food processor (or with a hand-held electric whisk), cream together the butter and sugar until light and fluffy. Beat 3 eggs and add to the mixture. Whizz together. Add 4 tbsp of the flour. Whizz. Add the last 3 eggs, beaten together. Whizz. Add the rest of the flour. Whizz. That's your cake batter. Pour it into the cake tin. Scatter over the chopped rhubarb. (Don't mix it in, as it would all sink to the bottom. This way it distributes itself evenly through the cake as it cooks.)

For the crumble topping, pulse together the butter and flour in a food processor or mix with your fingertips. Think crumbs, rather than a ball. Pour the crumbs over the rhubarb and sprinkle over the sugar.

Bake for 60–90 minutes. After 30 minutes, turn the oven down to about 160°C/325°F/gas mark 3 so that the outside doesn't get too crispy whilst the middle cooks. If you think the top is browning too quickly, place a piece of greaseproof paper over the top. The cake is cooked when a knife inserted in the middle comes out clean. (Make sure you don't pierce a piece of fruit, as this will give a false positive.) The crumble topping will not colour very much, so do not use this as a guide for done-ness.

MY FAVOURITE SPARKLING WINES

Laurent-Perrier Cuvée Rosé
My favourite pink Champagne (I drank it to celebrate writing this book).

Bollinger Special Cuvée
Full-bodied and gently sparkling, this is a very grown-up wine.

Nyetimber Classic Cuvée 2009
This sparkling wine from a vineyard in the South Downs is a wonderful way to celebrate British winemaking.

PARTIES

I used to get my knickers in a terrible twist when the prospect of entertaining more than a few people loomed. It took me several years of self-flagellation before I understood that people just want to feel looked after at a party, so I stopped trying to impress with fiddly canapés or complicated menus for twenty, and concentrated more on doing one or two things properly. (As well as making sure there was plenty of space for coats, lots of ice, soft drinks and loo roll, and a cracking party playlist.)

In this chapter you'll find my tried-and-tested plan for a cocktail party (see page 173) where the food on offer is chicken pie and a pile of brownies, and plenty of suggestions for simple party food to serve lots of people, much of which can be prepped in advance, as well as my top tips for party-throwing.

Balancing the requirements of guests, food and drink can be tricky, which is why planning everything in advance is the most important part of your organisation. You'll be surprised how much calmer you'll be when the event finally rolls around.

I've also included some of my favourite interactive meals in this chapter – and by that I mean big dishes of food into which everyone can dive, and recipes that get everyone involved in making up their own food: think Bang Bang Chicken (see page 179) or DIY Salmon and Vegetable Parcels (see page 182). They involve a bit of prep but their genius is that the host or hostess isn't chained to the kitchen.

PARTY TIPS

- Fill the bath with ice and water as a temporary ice bucket
- You will always need more ice than you think
- Start chilling the wine and Champagne the day before
- Buy the alcohol on sale or return
- Ban red wine
- Have empty cardboard boxes stashed away for all the empties
- Buy extra corkscrews if you are serving wine – someone WILL lose the only one
- Don't serve anything with tomato in: spills never come out
- Avoid candles: conflagrations are not chic
- Prime the neighbours
- Make sure you have enough cash to pay helpers
- And for the biggest party luxury: book your cleaning lady for the next morning

FIVE COCKTAILS IN JUGS

As a guide, I generally estimate a generous 50ml alcohol per head for a mixed cocktail. Most standard-sized glass jugs have a capacity of between 1.25 and 1.5 litres. Recipes below fill one cocktail jug, serving five to six, depending on how much ice you use. Note: 'muddling' means to crush together herbs and sugar using a 'muddler' or spoon, to release the aromatic oils.

LEMON, THYME AND VODKA

This cocktail is shaken not stirred, so you'll need to make a couple of batches to fill your jug. (The shaking is important as it bruises the herb and infuses its natural oil into the vodka.)

2 sprigs of fresh thyme, plus extra to garnish
1750ml vodka (or lemon vodka
  if you have it)
ice cubes
75ml Limoncello
75ml lemon juice
sparkling or soda water

Pick off the thyme leaves and add with the vodka to a cocktail shaker. Add a few cubes of ice, and make like Tom Cruise for a minute or so. Strain into a jug and add the Limoncello and lemon juice. Top up with sparkling or soda water. Serve in a highball. Garnish with a thyme sprig.

ELDERFLOWER, MINT, GIN AND CUCUMBER

ice cubes
250ml gin
175ml elderflower cordial
1 cucumber, sliced
large handful mint leaves
sparkling or soda water

Place a handful of ice into a jug and pour over the gin and elderflower cordial. Add the cucumber and mint and top up with sparkling water. Stir vigorously. Serve in a highball.

RASPBERRY MARTINIS

2 x 300g tins raspberries in syrup
  (not natural juice)
50ml Chambord or crème de framboise
200ml vodka, ideally from the freezer
ice cubes

Tip the raspberries and their syrup into a blender and whizz. Mix the Chambord or crème de framboise with the chilled vodka and raspberry juice. Fill one-third of a glass jug with ice cubes, pour in the cocktail and strain into a Martini glass.

A NOD TO AN 'OLD-FASHIONED': WHISKY AND BITTERS

50g caster sugar
10 dashes Angostura Bitters
250ml whisky
75ml orange juice (blood orange is
  particularly good)
ice cubes
orange zest strips and 1 maraschino cherry
  per cocktail, to garnish

Muddle together the sugar and the bitters, then add the whisky and orange juice and stir. Fill one-third of a jug with ice cubes, then pour in the cocktail. Serve immediately, strained into in a tumbler. Garnish with the zest and cherry.

PINK WHIPPET (NAMED IN HONOUR OF MY MOTHER'S WHIPPET, BILLY)

25g caster sugar
1 large handful mint leaves, plus extra
  to garnish
1 litre pink grapefruit juice
250ml vodka
ice cubes

Muddle together the sugar, mint leaves and grapefruit juice, then add the vodka. Fill one-third of a jug with ice cubes, then pour in the cocktail. Serve immediately, strained into a martini glass and garnished with mint.

BUTTERNUT SQUASH PURÉE FOR SCEPTICS

When I moved to the US, I was amazed at the prevalence of dips, especially quite substantial ones. (In the UK they are always quite liquid.) One of the things I really like about American parties at home are the wonderful, big bowls of dips that friends bring over for gatherings both large and small, whether or not they've been asked to bring food.

In New York or San Francisco, it was perfectly normal for a girlfriend to rock up to my front door for a TV party with a snazzy, multi-layered dip – almost a meal in itself and made according to a honed family recipe.

There certainly isn't a UK equivalent of this particularly US tradition and you won't find them in very many British cookbooks. They just aren't taken that seriously here; most often they lurk in tiny plastic pots in the chill section of the supermarket.

The first thing to acknowledge about the whole dippage thing is that they are very rarely bursting with goodness – unless your view of goodness is all about sour cream, cheese and a zillion calories, in which case your luck is so in.

The second is that dips aren't just something delicious whizzed up in the food processor in seconds (although that kind, like my Butter Bean and Thyme dip – see photo on page 168 – are excellent too): they are layered, they are often baked like my Artichoke and Spinach Dip (see page 169), and they are all sorts of yummy.

This butternut squash purée is one of those dishes that requires so little effort on the part of the cook, yet looks wonderful – perfect as a dip before supper starts. It would also be a great addition to a mezze.

I've discovered that it is also a crafty way to serve squash to the naysayers: there's something about the addition of the creamy cheese and the seeds that makes it look a whole lot more appealing than your average bowl of orange pap.

It has just three processes, the steaming of the squash, its purée-ing and the whipping of the cheese. What could be easier? (You do need a food processor for this dish.)

The purée is delicious served either hot or cold.

SECRET

Pumpkin oil is perfect for the garnish, but it's not always easy – or cheap – to find, so you can replace it with any oil with a distinct flavour. I like walnut or hazelnut, but a lovely, grassy Greek olive oil would be delicious here, too.

MAKES 1 LARGE BOWL
1 butternut squash
olive oil
sea salt and freshly ground
** black pepper**
125g ricotta cheese
1 tbsp pumpkin seeds and
** pumpkin oil (or other oil with**
** distinct flavour), to garnish**

METHOD
Roughly chop the squash into
small chunks, removing the
seeds, and steam over a pan of
boiling water for approximately
20 minutes.

When soft, scoop the flesh
away from the skin into a food
processor bowl and pulse with a
drizzle of olive oil and a pinch of
salt, until a purée forms.

Tip the ricotta into a bowl, add a
pinch of salt and a grind of black
pepper. Whip together briefly
with a fork.

To serve, spoon the purée into a
flattish bowl and carefully spoon
the cheese into the middle,
flattening it with the back of the
spoon. Sprinkle over the seeds
and drizzle over some oil.

THE HOLIDAY SEASON PARTY

Whether your idea of a holiday season party is hosting three
hundred of your closest friends in a ballroom, or having ten
friends over for mulled wine and a kitchen supper, there are
some tricks to make the whole shebang simpler.

Send out the invitations well in advance. That way, if
people get a better offer, hopefully they will honour your
request – even if they come to you first and move on. I like
Paperless Post online, which allows you to send reminders
and track RSVPs.

Don't overthink the decor: there is always the temptation
to go all out at Christmas and, whilst I am a fan of the over-
the-top event, I say save it for the rest of the year. Christmas
decorations are wonderful, so I like to stay traditional, but
you can always play with the colour scheme if you really
must be different. How about a pink tree this year?

People always eat and drink everything in sight at a
holiday party. (I think they are preparing for the boredom
of January by building up fat stocks.) So, if you have limited
supplies or a limited time frame, come up with a plan
for politely getting people to move on to the next party,
without making them feel like they are being booted out.
(Turning the music down is always a good start.)

Speaking of music, a good playlist is vital. In the fluster of
getting everything else organised, I always forget it. Make
the music a priority – and if you don't have time, flatter a
friend into doing it. Something along the lines of, 'You have
such amazing taste in music! Do you think ... etc, etc?'

Don't forget to tell the neighbours if your party is at
home. Ideally, invite them, too, and ply them with drinks,
so they can't complain if it gets a bit noisy later.

Most importantly of all, remember that the secret to
hosting a good party is to enjoy yourself.

Chickpeas and flat-leaf parsley (try adding 1 tbsp tahini and thin with warm water, to make hummus)

Chickpea, lemon, black olive, 5 tbsp olive oil, 100g olives, a squeeze of lemon, and flat-leaf parsley

Butter bean and thyme

BEAN PUREES

Anyone can whizz up a purée of beans or vegetables with olive oil, garlic and herbs. It's a useful trick to know for parties: the purées can be made in advance, covered in clingfilm, refrigerated and then perked up with a slosh of olive oil and a scattering of herbs. Take out of the fridge an hour or so before you intend to eat.

The technique is easy: drain a tin of pulses and dump into a food processor, along with a fat clove of garlic, a good pinch of salt and some black pepper. Add a tablespoon of olive oil, and whizz together until combined. Add some soft herbs for green flecks; or chilli flakes for heat. Experiment with amounts of oil: a tablespoon will give you a very rough texture; 4–6 tablespoons poured through the lid funnel as you whizz will give you a very smooth, almost silky texture. Equally, use some of the liquid that the beans were tinned in instead of the extra oil.

My favourite combinations are in the photo opposite. Others you can try are cannellini bean with a little Sriracha chilli sauce; roasted carrots puréed with cumin; roasted white onions puréed with ground coriander and coriander leaves.

SUPERBOWL AVOCADO AND BEAN DIP

I cannot pretend to understand American Football but, when the annual Superbowl comes around, I see it as an excuse to eat vast quantities of dips and chips. So, in honour of the Superbowl and my dear friend in Chicago, the wonderful Jill, who knows as much about football as I do about fashion, here is my Superbowl Dip. It's based on nachos, but designed for easier scooping.

SERVES 6–8
refried beans
grated cheese (Monterey Jack or Cheddar)
chopped olives
tomato salsa
a dash of hot sauce (such as Tabasco)
sour cream
Four-Minute Guacamole, to serve (see page 170)

METHOD
Preheat the oven to 180°C/350°F/gas mark 4. In a large ovenproof dish, spoon the beans, cover with grated cheese, then olives, salsa, hot sauce and sour cream. Cover the whole lot with grated cheese. Pop in the oven for 10–15 minutes until it is warmed through and the cheese has melted. Spread more sour cream over the top, then smooth a layer of guacamole over it with the back of a spoon. Use salted tortilla chips for dipping. (Try not to spill down your front.)

ARTICHOKE AND SPINACH DIP

One of my favourite dips is the American classic, artichoke and spinach, a dip that I have never seen over on the English side of the Atlantic. I first had it in an East Village bar in New York, and was speechless at its moreishness. It's a baked dip, so served hot, and is rich with tangy artichokes, cheese, cream and spinach.

SERVES 6–8
200g cream cheese
50g Parmesan, finely grated
150g sour cream
2 tbsp mayonnaise (this is optional, but do not use a reduced-fat version, as it may split)
200g frozen, chopped spinach, thawed
240g artichoke hearts (approx. 400g undrained weight), drained and finely chopped
sea salt and freshly ground black pepper

METHOD
Preheat the oven to 180°C/350°F/gas mark 4. Tip the cream cheese, Parmesan, sour cream and mayo into a big bowl and stir until thoroughly mixed. Mix in the spinach and artichokes. Grind over lots of black pepper and add salt to taste. Tip into an ovenproof bowl and bake for around 20 minutes. Excellent with tortilla chips, pitta or carrot sticks.

FOUR-MINUTE GUACAMOLE

There are as many ways to make guacamole as there are varieties of avocado in Mexico. I'm not pretending that this is an authentic version, but it's still delicious. And, best of all it takes maybe four minutes. Sold? I knew you would be.

Ideally, this is pounded with a pestle in a large mortar – the nearest we have in the UK to the *molcajete* in which guacamole is traditionally made. Otherwise, a bowl and the back of a fork will suffice.

SERVES 6
2 large avocados (or 4 of those baby ones)
dash of hot sauce (Tabasco is good)
½ red onion, finely chopped
1 tbsp lime juice (or lemon)
good pinch of sea salt
1 small tomato, very finely chopped
1 leafy coriander sprig, finely chopped, with stalk included

METHOD
Halve the avocados and scoop out the flesh into a mortar (or a bowl).

Add the dash of hot sauce, red onion, lime juice, salt, tomato and coriander.

Pound it all together with a pestle or fork. Guacamole is supposed to be chunky, so don't reduce it to pulp.

Eat with chips, or crudités, if you are inclined towards healthy eating.

Do not make in advance: guacamole is all about the fresh flavours, and it will go brown.

PIMIENTOS DE PADRÓN FRITOS

Oh, I have much love for *pimientos de Padrón fritos*. Originating from Padrón in Galicia, in the north-west corner of Spain, the dish is a trinity of little green peppers, olive oil and sea salt. It takes a matter of minutes to get from a rinse under the tap to being showered with sea salt on the plate, via a frying pan of hot oil. The perfect TV snack: no carbs, but ever so more-ish and good.

However, although they do appear to be the simplest possible snack, they come with a built-in surprise. These deceptive little peppers are the Russian roulette of vegetables: for every five or so you pop in your mouth, one will be super hot. I am taking this on trust, though, because, for all the plates of pimientos de Padrón I have eaten over the years, I have not yet had a hot one.

ALLOW 3–4 PEPPERS PER PERSON
splash of olive oil
handful Padrón peppers
coarse sea salt

METHOD
Heat up some standard olive oil in a frying pan, tip in your peppers and cook over a high heat until they begin to blister and blacken.

When you tip them out onto some kitchen paper they will immediately deflate.

Sprinkle them with sea salt and eat with your fingers (don't eat the stalks).

Eat, as I did in Jerez recently, accompanied by a lovely, chilled glass of Fino sherry.

SUPER-LONG CHEESE STRAWS

A cheese straw is a pleasing thing. Although possibly best eaten at parties over wooden floors, rather than carpets, as they do tend to shower flakes of pastry everywhere.

Whilst it is more normal to make them quite short, for parties I like to make them about a foot long (that's 30cm) and place them in (well-scrubbed) glass vases. There's a practical reason for this: vases don't just look good, they are weighted at the base, so they don't topple over when flowers are placed in them. Because these straws are so long, you don't want the delicate pastry crashing to the floor.

MAKES APPROX. 10

100g Parmesan, grated
25g English mustard powder
flour, for dusting
500g ready-made, rolled all-butter puff pastry
1 egg, lightly beaten
3 baking trays, greased

METHOD
Preheat the oven to 180°C/350°F/gas mark 4.

Mix the Parmesan with the mustard powder.

Sprinkle flour over the work surface and unroll the pastry. Roll it out with a rolling pin, if necessary, to get it about 0.25cm thick. Scatter half the Parmesan mixture over half the pastry and fold over. Roll out once more with the rolling pin. Cut the pastry into long strips about 2cm wide.

Brush each strip with the beaten egg, then sprinkle the rest of the Parmesan mixture over each one.

Transfer each strip to the baking trays, twisting it twice as you lay it down. Bake for approximately 15 minutes until puffed up and golden. Remove to a wire rack to cool.

DELICIOUS LITTLE THINGS ON TOAST

JAMON, MOZZARELLA AND BASIL ON WALNUT BREAD

Brush slices of walnut bread with olive oil and toast under the grill on each side for a few minutes. Cut the toasted bread into fingers, place a basil leaf on each one, then a strip of jamón, followed by a small piece of mozzarella.

FIGS AND PROSCIUTTO ON SOURDOUGH

Oil and toast bread as above, lay on the prosciutto, then top with fig quarters.

MUSHROOM, CHIVE AND CREAM CHEESE ON GRANARY

Blitz 500g mushrooms in a food processor, then fry in 1 tbsp butter until soft and the juices have evaporated. Tip into a bowl and mix with 150g cream cheese and some finely snipped chives. Pile onto toasted granary. Grind over black pepper.

ARTICHOKE PASTE ON SOURDOUGH

Whizz a jar of artichokes with their oil in a food processor, check seasoning and spread on oiled and toasted sourdough.

SECRET
My mother always used to serve what seemed like hundreds of the goat's cheese toasts at drinks parties; one of her tricks was to slice and toast the bread rounds in advance, put them in the freezer until needed, then pop them under the grill still frozen.

GOAT'S CHEESE WITH PX ON TOAST

PX is short for Pedro Ximénez, one of the richest, most delicious sherries, and the raisin-y sweetness is fantastic against the sharp, creamy tang of goat's cheese. Serve these as party snacks, or three at a time with some salad for a starter or light lunch. Ideally, you need to use a *bûche de chèvre*, the narrow logs of goat's cheese with a rind, which come wrapped in plastic-covered paper. You could use a spreadable goat's cheese, but you won't get the lovely, melted gooeyness that comes from a cheese with a rind.

They are best made using a *ficelle* (the slightly slimmer form of baguette), so you get a good ratio of cheese to bread.

SERVES 8–12 AS PARTY SNACKS
2 bûches de chèvre
2 ficelles
50ml Pedro Ximénez sherry

METHOD

Unwrap the cheese and slice into 1cm rounds. It's easiest to use a serrated or bread knife, to prevent the cheese sticking.

Turn on the grill to high. Slice the bread into 1cm thick rounds and grill on one side until golden. Flip over the rounds, place a piece of cheese on each one and return to the grill.

When the cheese is bubbling, remove from the grill and brush sherry over each round.

Either slide onto boards, or serve on plates with watercress and lettuce.

THE COCKTAILS
AND PIE PARTY

My birthday falls at the beginning of December. For someone who loves to throw a party, this is not exactly ideal, given that it's party month. Even if people aren't flitting from event to event, they are likely to be wound up with the excitement and stress of preparing for the Christmas season.

On the other hand, my birthday is early enough to kick off the holiday season. After a few parties that I have filed under 'trial and error', I have finally got my perfect holiday party recipe down pat.

The most important thing is to make sure that you don't leave yourself with too much to do during the party itself: the key to a good time is preparation, preparation, preparation.

The first thing I learnt was, no fiddly canapés. For my thirtieth I had planned a menu of trays of simple little things to eat, but hadn't given much thought to how they were going to be assembled during the actual party. I didn't have any help in the kitchen, bar my flatmate, and it was all a little bit disastrous. I had also planned that my boyfriend and I would serve all the drinks. No, that didn't really work either. Because someone needs to answer the door, take coats and welcome guests.

I learnt my lesson from that event: henceforth I would always have somebody to help me with, well, everything. If you are partner-free, then two people. So the most important thing is to secure your help well in advance. I recommend asking at your local bar for recommendations.

Drinks-wise, it's best to keep it simple. No one really likes punch after university (and did we even like it then?) and, unless you are standing outside to watch fireworks or sing carols, resist the temptation to serve mulled wine.

I usually serve cocktails and Champagne or prosecco only, having searched around online for the best deal and then having the retailer deliver it to me, to save me hefting it into the house. I ban red wine: there's always a spillage disaster however hard you try to contain it.

Whilst I love the idea of having somebody doing a Tom Cruise and shaking individually made cocktails over their shoulder, in reality it is not very practical if you've only got one bar person and fifty people desperate for a drink. So what we do is stick to one spirit, usually vodka (because most people drink it), and make up several jugs of cocktails in advance. (A pre-party cocktail-tasting supper, a week or so before, is clearly vital.)

Ice in large quantity is essential – keep it in the bath if necessary. Serve the pre mixed cocktails over ice in a highball, or shake them up with ice on demand. Place buckets filled with ice and water under the bar table for the Champagne or prosecco.

Don't forget that you'll need plenty of soft drinks: my favourite is huge jugs of elderflower cordial with lots of mint and ice to make them look pretty.

After my canapé disaster, I decided to stop serving fiddly food that gets ground into carpets, and to make pies. Yes, pies. For about a hundred people, I make five giant chicken-and-vegetable pies (see page 175) and one Quorn-and-mushroom one, in roasting tins, the day before.

This is my idea of perfect party food: the already made pies go in the oven around 7.30pm to warm through. Everybody arrives at about 8pm after work either because they took too long getting ready or because they are waiting for a babysitter. At around 9pm when everyone has had plenty of cocktails and is feeling pretty peckish, we dish up the pies onto paper plates. Everybody dives in: honestly, they couldn't be happier (who doesn't like pie?) and the best bit is that all the paper plates and plastic forks go straight into the bin, and there is no washing up.

Then, a while later, I hand around great piles of brownies (see page 150), which I have cut up in advance and clingfilmed.

Result: very happy guests and (almost) stress-free host.

GIANT CHICKEN PIE

Making a large pie can seem daunting but, wonderfully, it's actually rather simple, requiring nothing more complicated than a standard roasting tin. I chose the tin, as opposed to a traditional china dish, for two reasons: when I first threw a party for 100 people and wanted to feed everyone pie, I needed five or six identical dishes, and that presented two problems: cost, and storage afterwards. Then I hit on the idea of using metal roasting tins because they can be picked up for a few pounds each and they stack together. They also conduct heat beautifully, so your pie hots up rapidly.

Using a roasting tin does mean the pie isn't particularly deep, but when you are catering for the masses, you want more acreage than depth, more pastry than filling, otherwise portion control can be tricky. (Those lovely blackbird pie funnels, traditionally used in deep pies to let the steam out and stop the lid sinking, are more for decoration here than utility.)

SERVES 12–15

For the poached chicken
1 large, organic, free-range
  chicken (around 1.2–1.5kg)
1 carrot
1 onion
1 leek

For the pie
500g white mushrooms,
  quartered
4 leeks, thickly sliced
2 tbsp olive oil
4 carrots, cut into chunks
100g plain flour, plus extra
  for dusting
2 x 375g packets ready-made,
  rolled puff pastry
100g butter
1 tbsp Dijon mustard
1 litre hot liquid (preferably
  500ml chicken stock and
  500ml milk)
250g grated cheese (preferably
  Cheddar)
1 egg, lightly beaten
large roasting tin

METHOD

Follow the instructions for poaching the chicken on page 73, straining and reserving the cooking liquid. Remove the meat from the bones (discarding the bones) and cut into bite-size pieces.

For the pie, fry the mushrooms and the leeks separately in 1 tbsp olive oil each and steam or boil the carrots until al dente. Set aside.

Sprinkle flour over the work surface and unroll one packet of pastry. Using the top of the roasting tin as a template, roll out the pastry further with a rolling pin (being careful not to roll it too thin) until it's big enough to fit over the tin. Unroll the second packet of pastry and cut long strips the width and length of the lip of the roasting tin sides, to cover each side. Cover with a tea towel.

Using the butter, 100g flour, the mustard and hot liquid, make the white sauce according to the instructions on page 73, adding in the grated cheese at the end and stirring until melted through.

Tip the mushrooms, leeks and carrots into the roasting tin, being careful not to add the cooking liquid, as this will make the sauce too runny and cause it to separate. Add the chicken and distribute evenly. Pour the white sauce over the chicken and vegetables, making sure it is all mixed in. If you are using blackbird pie funnels, place these now. Leave to cool slightly. Preheat the oven to 180°C/350°F/gas mark 4.

Flip the large piece of pastry over the roasting tin, using a small sharp knife to make a cross where each blackbird will poke through. Do not worry if the pastry doesn't quite stretch over the lip of the tin. Brush the beaten egg over the edges and place the pastry strips, cut earlier, over the lip of the tin to secure the pastry sheet on all sides. Brush the entire top of the pie with beaten egg.

Bake for about 25 minutes, or until the pastry is risen and golden.

BOARDS OF GOOD THINGS

I like to finish off a meal by plonking a wooden board in the middle of the table. On it will be something delicious to pick at while the conversation flows. Perhaps cheese and good bread, or maybe a selection of sweet things I have picked up on my travels. Boards of good things are great for parties, too: easy to hand around, unbreakable and aesthetically pleasing.

There's a common fallacy that says serving up things you haven't made yourself is cheating somehow. I say pah! to that: whilst I would never give a ready meal to anyone except myself (yes, sometimes the microwave is my friend), there's nothing wrong in saving yourself stress by not making everything, or skipping a course.

The most obvious thing that looks wonderful on a large board is a gorgeous, large piece of cheese. Unless you are catering for fifteen-plus people, I think it's a bit of a waste to serve up more than two types as, invariably, you will be

left with clingfilm-wrapped pieces which lurk in the back of the fridge. Instead, invest in a showstopper piece of runny cheese such as Brie or Epoisses; or a huge hunk of hard cheese such as a farmhouse Cheddar or Wensleydale. Add grapes, dried apricots, chutney or membrillo.

When I am abroad I always try to find a local store to pick up local, sweet specialities for my storecupboard. I also do a supermarket sweep around duty-free shops when I haven't had time to go anywhere beyond hotel and meetings: even the Eurostar terminal at Gare du Nord has turned up trumps before, and it's handy having a stockpile for emergency entertaining.

These sweet things might include several types of turrón; pretty, pastel-coloured Turkish delight; amaretti biscuits in delicate tissue wrappers; sticky Medjool dates; broken-off pieces of panforte di Siena; biscotti; marrons glacés and macaroons.

Delicious Things
to Buy in Spain

Spain's markets are packed full of ingredients that any greedy cook will long to buy. Fortunately you can bring any fruit, vegetables, meat, dairy or other animal products (such as fish, eggs and honey) into the UK if you're travelling from a country within the EU so, if you have room in your luggage, the only issue will be the size of your bag – and your wallet.

If I have room in my hand luggage, I buy tomatoes – Spanish ones are the best in the world – and in the autumn I look for interesting mushrooms.

My favourite Spanish market is the nineteenth-century Mercat de Sant Josep de la Boqueria on Barcelona's Ramblas (see right).

Even if I only have a few spare minutes in the city, I always try to buy a selection of technicoloured glacé fruits from one of the many specialists in the Boqueria. They are wonderful as an after-dinner treat, used in Christmas cake, or chopped into ice cream to make scrumptious tutti frutti.

I always try to go home with some of the following:

- Pimientos de Padrón
- Dried chillies
- Chorizo sausages
- Jamón serrano
- Salted Marcona almonds
- Turrón – the chewy Spanish nougat, which is especially good covered in chocolate
- Polvorones – crumbly almond biscuits
- Glacé fruits

Spanish Markets to Look out for

Mercat de Sant Josep de la Boqueria (also known as La Boqueria) on Barcelona's Ramblas; open Monday to Saturday 8am to 8.30pm; www.boqueria.info

Mercado Central de Abastos, Plaza de Abastos, Jerez de la Frontera; www.jerez.es

Mercado de San Miguel, Plaza de San Miguel, Madrid; open Monday to Wednesday and Sunday, 10am to midnight; Thursday to Saturday, 10am to 2pm; www.mercadodesanmiguel.es

BANG BANG CHICKEN

I don't just love this dish because of its name (which is irresistibly good and comes from the noise made when cooks would tenderise the chicken by banging it with a mallet) but because it is as finger-lickin' good as it is easy. It's so simple that it would be a great recipe to make with children, although there is nothing childish about it. It originates from Sichuan, where the inclusion of Sichuan peppercorn makes it a much fierier dish than we eat in the West. (Feel free to add 1 or 2 tsp if you crave the burn.)

Bang bang chicken is usually served with its sauce over noodles – either rice or mung bean – but I like to serve mine as a DIY version with all the ingredients separated so the eaters can choose their favourite combination to roll up in a pancake.

I first made this for a Shrove Tuesday supper party, which I didn't want to feel like a one-note meal, so I used a different kind of pancake for each course. The ones I use to wrap the chicken in are the thin, rice versions that you can find in any Asian supermarket, often in the freezer section. They are inexpensive and are packaged so that you can just remove what you need and pop the others back in the freezer. (I find them very useful for last-minute suppers.)

SERVES 6
6 chicken breasts (on the bone)
200g rice noodles
sesame oil

For the sauce
8 tbsp peanut butter (either smooth or crunchy)
6 tbsp sweet chilli sauce
2 tsp lime juice
2 tbsp soy sauce
2 tbsp rice vinegar
2 tbsp sesame oil

For the table
4 rice pancakes per head, plus a few extra (about 30)
3 tbsp sesame seeds
200g beansprouts
2 carrots (optional)
2 baby gem lettuces
bunch spring onions
1 cucumber
½ bunch coriander

METHOD

Rinse the chicken breasts under a running tap. Put them in a saucepan, cover with cold water and place over a medium heat. Bring to a simmer and poach gently for 15 minutes. Check the inside of a breast, and if there is any hint of pinkness, simmer for another 5 minutes or until cooked through.

When the chicken is cooked, remove from the water, take off the skin and discard. Reserve the poaching liquid. Pull the meat from the bone and shred neatly – you can use a fork or your fingers.

Dump the sauce ingredients in another pan with 240ml of the reserved poaching liquid. Mix thoroughly and heat over a gentle flame to warm through. (Do not to let it catch – burnt peanuts smell revolting.)

Plunge the rice noodles into a pan of boiling water. They should cook almost immediately but do check packet instructions. Drain, then add a drop of sesame oil to stop them sticking together.

If you have a steamer, place it over a pan of simmering water and add the pancakes to the basket to warm through. Otherwise, they can be wrapped in foil and warmed in the oven.

Heat a frying pan and pour in the sesame seeds to toast for 30 seconds. (This is optional, but they taste better toasted.)

For the table, rinse the beansprouts, grate the carrots, if using, separate the lettuce leaves, shred the onions and cut the cucumber into matchsticks.

Arrange the chicken, noodles, pancakes, vegetables and coriander on a series of plates. Pour the sauce into 2 bowls. Put the sesame seeds in a little bowl. Let everyone assemble their own pancakes at the table. Don't forget lots of napkins, as the sauce drips down chins and fingers.

(If you are making this on a hot summer day, don't heat the sauce, and allow the chicken and the noodles to cool to room temperature.)

DIY SALMON AND VEGETABLE PARCELS
WITH LEMON AND CREAM SAUCE

There is something very beguiling about brown paper packages tied up with string – as we all know from the song. And, whilst I'm always happy to find a present inside, a delicious meal is equally welcome.

I first came across this way of serving food *en papillote* at a very smart lunch in a marquee. Running down the centre of the table were pots of soft green herbs, and each place setting had a little jug of creamy sauce and a pair of scissors. The idea was that we would open up our parcels, pour over the sauce and snip the herbs of our choice over the top. It's a lovely idea, and easily replicated at home with little fuss. I cook both salmon and vegetables this way and, even if there are no vegetarians around, cook several green parcels as well, to accompany the fish.

METHOD
Preheat the oven to 180°C/350°F/gas mark 4.

For the lemon and cream sauce, cook the shallot, lemon juice and wine together at a gentle simmer for 10–15 minutes until it has reduced by half. Add the cream and cook for a further 5 minutes. Add the butter cubes to the sauce, piece by piece, vigorously whisking each time until all the butter is combined. Do be careful it doesn't catch.

Place the salmon fillet or the vegetables in the middle of a square of greaseproof paper and add a knob of butter and a splash of white wine. Wrap up the parchment to form a parcel. Secure with string, repeat with the remaining salmon and vegetables, and place on a large baking tray in the oven. Cook for about 10 minutes. Use a fish slice to remove the parcels from the baking tray, as the liquid inside will make the parcels floppy.

Serve the parcels on a large platter in the middle of the table for everyone to help themselves. Then they can snip their own herbs, squeeze over a lemon wedge, and pour over the lemon and cream sauce.

SERVES 4

For the lemon and cream sauce
1 shallot, very finely chopped
juice of 2 lemons
a little white wine
250ml single cream
250g butter, cubed

For the fish parcels
1 salmon fillet per person
a little butter
a little white wine
greaseproof paper
kitchen string

For the vegetable parcels
petits pois, mangetout, sugar snap peas, green beans, trimmed asparagus, julienned carrots, courgettes, and fennel
a little butter
a little white wine
greaseproof paper
kitchen string

For the table
fresh chervil, chives, tarragon, flat-leaf parsley, thyme, oregano, dill
lemon wedges

BAKED CAMEMBERT
WITH HERBS AND ROASTED SPRING ONIONS

Is this a recipe? I think that's probably pushing it. What it is, is a brilliant way of turning unripe Camembert – the type that seems to have a Styrofoam middle – into a meltingly unctuous dish that far transcends its rather dull origins.

A couple of these are perfect to plonk on the table pre-supper, when guests arrive ravenous, but food isn't quite ready. Or else, you can serve one each as a main course alongside some good bread or a bowl of boiled potatoes. Cornichons are a perfect accompaniment.

Any sprigs of herbs will do: rosemary or thyme are lovely; equally, marjoram and oregano work well. You could also try trickling over some honey, as its sweetness contrasts beautifully with the salty, creamy cheese.

I like to accompany the cheese with bunches of spring onions, roasted in the oven at the same time. Do make sure you buy the Camemberts in wooden boxes, not cardboard ones, as the latter will leak molten goop.

SERVES 2–6, DEPENDING ON HUNGER LEVELS
1 bunch spring onions
1 tbsp olive oil, plus more
   for drizzling
1 Camembert in a wooden box
few sprigs of herbs

METHOD
Preheat the oven to 180°C/350°F/gas mark 4.

Top and tail the spring onions and place in an ovenproof dish with the oil and toss together.

Unwrap the Camembert and discard the lid of the box. Make 3 slits in the cheese, poke in sprigs of herbs and drizzle over some olive oil to keep the crust supple during the cooking.

Whack the boxed cheese in the oven, alongside the spring onions, in a big dish for about 15 minutes. (Do not ever bake just in their boxes. You are risking a big molten-cheese mess on the floor of your oven.)

The spring onions will need about 20 minutes altogether, or until soft with crispy – even blackened – ends.

QUESO FUNDIDO

I always love the idea of sitting around a big steaming dish of food, into which we can all dive, elbows out and forks in – and if it involves melted cheese, then so much the better.

Queso fundido (meaning 'melted cheese') is the Mexican cousin of Swiss fondue. Although you don't dip anything in the cheese, it does make sense to keep it warming over a lamp or tea light, as you would a fondue, so that the cheese doesn't seize and separate.

If you can order from one of the great specialist suppliers online, it's worth trying to track down some of the traditional cheeses that are used to make this dish, including Oaxaca and Chihuahua. However, the rest of us can get by just fine using a mixture of mozzarella and Cheddar. I've had the best results using those bags of pre-grated mozzarella, as they melt evenly, and occasionally I've been lucky enough to find a grated mix also containing Monterey Jack, an American cheese that melts perfectly and would always be my first choice.

> ## SECRET
> For a vegetarian variation, omit the chorizo, heat a knob of butter and add a crushed garlic clove and 300g sliced mushrooms to the sizzling fat. Cook until soft and tip over the bubbling cheese.

SERVES 4–6

200g chorizo, crumbled out of its casing (it may need to be finely chopped)

4 tomatoes

1 medium onion, chopped

1 large garlic clove, finely chopped

500g grated cheese (my basic mix is 250g grated mozzarella cheese plus 250g grated Cheddar or Monterey Jack, if you can find it. If I have some Manchego left over from a party, then I sub that in, too. Mmm.)

handful coriander leaves

corn tortilla chips or large tortillas, to serve

large ovenproof frying pan, preferably cast-iron

METHOD

Place a frying pan over a medium-high heat. Crumble in the chorizo. (Do not add any extra oil: it gives off plenty.) Cook for about 5 minutes, until it starts to give off its characteristic red oil. Then remove the chorizo with a slotted spoon to a plate, leaving the oil in the pan.

Whilst the chorizo is cooking, chop the tomatoes into small pieces.

Keep the pan over the heat but turn it down to medium. Add the chopped onion and cook until translucent. This will take at least 15 minutes. When the onion is done, add the garlic and cook for a few minutes. Then tip the chorizo back in the pan, make sure everything is mixed together and keep warm over a very low heat.

Meanwhile, preheat the oven to 180°C/350°F/gas mark 4. Mix the cheeses together and add to the cast-iron frying pan. Stick in the oven for 5–10 minutes, but keep a beady eye on the cheese: you don't want it starting to separate. (The aim is a pan of molten deliciousness.) Remove the pan from the oven and spoon the warm chorizo-onion mixture in the middle.

Heap over the chopped tomatoes and scatter lots of coriander over everything. Either dip tortilla chips into the melted cheese, or spoon the cheese onto large corn or wheat tortillas.

Favourite Florists

I love sending people flowers, and I love receiving them too, so I've always figured if sending them gives even half the joy I get from an unsolicited bunch of flowers, then it's money well spent.

These are the people from whom I order flowers around the world.

Paris: L'Artisan Fleuriste

Their beautiful, colour co-ordinated shop in the Marais is wonderful to visit, but their insistence on seasonal and usually French flowers makes for glorious bouquets too.

95 Rue Vieille du Temple, 75003 Paris

Sydney: Mr Cook

Order a massed bunch of just one bloom from Sean Cook for maximum impact.

318 New South Head Rd, Double Bay, Sydney, NSW 2028 www.mrcook.com.au

New York: Opalia Flowers

Beautiful Opalia in Boerum Hill designs the most ravishing vases – in season ask for their blowsy peonies – and delivers all over the five boroughs.

377 Atlantic Avenue, Brooklyn, NY 11217 www.opaliaflowers.com

UK: Rebel Rebel

I use Rebel Rebel to send flowers to my friends in East London and each time they come up with something perfectly bespoke for the recipient.

5 Broadway Market, London E8 4PH www.rebelrebel.co.uk

UK: Miss Pickering

Whether she uses herbs or flowers, Miss Pickering's scented arrangements are always a joy to behold. She also has a wonderful whippet guarding her shop.

7 St Paul's Street, Stamford PE9 2BE www.misspickering.com

ICE-CREAM SUNDAES

Why should ice-cream sundaes be just for children? There's a voluptuous pleasure in a loaded spoonful of ice cream, covered in a scrumptious sauce and loaded with nuts, topped with, maybe, a flump of whipped cream. Just make sure you forget shop-bought, luminous syrups; use proper chocolate in your sauce; fresh fruit, not tinned; and avoid squirty cream, which always disappointingly melts to a watery nothingness.

BANANA SPLIT
This is sundae simplicity at its best: take one banana, peel it, halve it lengthways, spoon vanilla ice cream down the middle, drizzle over hot chocolate sauce, cover in whipped cream and toasted almonds.

HOT FUDGE SUNDAE
Two scoops of vanilla ice cream, topped with hot fudge sauce, whipped cream, toasted almonds and a cherry on top.

HOT BROWNIE SUNDAE
A warm brownie (preferably straight from the oven – see page 150), on which are balanced two scoops of either vanilla or chocolate ice cream, butterscotch sauce, whipped cream and maple walnuts.

KNICKERBOCKER GLORY
Experts believe that a classic Knickerbocker is served in a tall glass, filled with layers of three scoops of different colours (traditionally strawberry, chocolate and vanilla), jelly, chopped fruit and nuts, chocolate sauce, strawberry sauce and toasted almonds. A cherry on the top, preferably one from a jar, is obligatory.

BROWN DERBY
A sugared ring doughnut, topped with a swirl of ice cream, chocolate sauce and chopped nuts appeared on Wimpy menus throughout my childhood. I was never allowed to order one, but I made up for the deprivation by constructing one recently. It was epic.

UNBEATABLE ACCOMPANIMENTS FOR VANILLA ICE CREAM
Blueberries and lemon curd

Strawberry purée, crushed meringue, flaked almonds

Hazelnut chocolate spread, chopped nuts, hot chocolate sauce

Mango purée, sliced peaches and whipped cream

GREAT SUNDAE TOPPINGS

Chocolate sauce

Butterscotch sauce

Marshmallow creme

Teeny, tiny marshmallows

Sprinkles

Hundreds and thousands

Chocolate chips

Honey

Maple syrup

Bananas

Whipped cream

Strawberry purée

Mango purée

Raspberry coulis

Sliced peaches

Chantilly cream

Chopped nuts

Flaked almonds

Candied walnuts

Berries (blueberries, chopped strawberries, raspberries, blackberries, blackcurrants)

Rose syrup

Hazelnut chocolate spread

Lemon curd

TOP PLACES TO INDULGE IN

Ice Cream
AND *Sundaes*
AROUND THE WORLD

UK

The Parlour Restaurant at Fortnum & Mason, 181 Piccadilly, London W1A 1ER

Gelupo, 7 Archer Street, London W1D 7AU

Chin Chin Laboratorists, 49–50 Camden Lock Place, London NW1 8AF

Marine Ices, 8 Haverstock Hill, London NW3 2BL

Ice Cream Parlour at Harrods, 2nd floor, Harrods, 87–135 Brompton Road, London SW1X 7XL

Roskilly Ice Cream, Tregellast Barton Farm, St Keverne, Helston, Cornwall TR12 6NX

Morelli's, 14 Victoria Parade, Broadstairs, Kent CT10 1QS

Nardini's Esplanade Café, 2 Greenock Rd, Largs, North Ayrshire KA30 8NF

USA

Serendipity 3, 225 East 60th Street, New York, NY 10022

Ici Ice Cream, 2948 College Avenue, Berkeley, CA 94705

The Ice Cream Bar, 815 Cole Street, Cole Valley, San Francisco, CA 94117

FRANCE

Berthillon, 31 rue Saint Louis en l'Île, 75004 Paris

SINGAPORE

Azabu Sabo, Food Court @ Takashimaya Department Store, 391 Orchard Road, Singapore 238873

INDEX

A

almonds: Brussels sprouts with 98
  plum and almond little cakes 151
the ambassador's cake 149
Amsterdam, flower markets 138
apples: apple sauce 97
  baked apples 139
  blackberry and apple trifle 126
  Eve's pudding, three ways 140
  infused hot apple juice 47
  cake 134–5
apricots, Eve's pudding with 140
artichokes: artichoke and spinach
  dip 169
  artichoke paste on sourdough
  toast 172
asparagus risotto with pea purée 104
avocados: avocado, grapefruit and
  red onion salad 60
  four-minute guacamole 170
  LibertyLondonGirl's salad 52
  Mexican salad 114
  sandwiches 111
  Superbowl avocado and bean 169

B

bacon: sweetcorn, cheese and bacon
  muffins 17
Bali, presents for godchildren 83
banana split 186
bang bang chicken 179
Bangkok, flea markets 93
Barcelona, presents for godchildren
  83
barley: courgette and pea orzotto 76
  winter-warming beef stew 41
Bath, fashion museums 63
beaches for picnics 112
beans: bean purées 168–9
  huevos rancheros 24
  lamb cutlets on mashed butter
  beans 88
  mushrooms on toast with white
  beans 79
  pork, chorizo and white bean
  stew 42
  Superbowl avocado and bean 169
beef: the perfect burger 28
  winter-warming beef stew 41
Berkeley, ice-cream parlours 187
Berlin, places to eat cake 159
berries: jewelled jellies in jars 119
  mixed berry summer pudding 123
  summer berry tart 131
birthday cake, ice-cream 156–9

biscuits see cookies
blackberries: blackberry and apple
  trifle 126
  fresh blackberry jam 146
blueberries: Eve's pudding with 140
  patriotic pavlova 124–5
boards of good things 176
bookshops for cooks 58
bouillon, vegetable 73
bread: French toast (eggy bread) 18
  mixed berry summer pudding 123
  puffed-up bread pudding with
  cheese and ham 43
  sandwiches 111
  see also toast
bread-and-butter pudding, hot-cross-
  bun 137
Bristol, flea markets 93
Broadstairs, ice-cream parlours 187
brocantes, French 14
brown Derby sundae 186
brownies 150
  hot brownie sundae 186
brunch, restaurants for 22
Brussels sprouts with almonds 98
buffalo mozzarella with blood
  oranges 55
burger sauce 31
burgers: cauliflower and quinoa
  burger 33
  Glamorgan burger 32
  mushroom and halloumi burger 31
  the perfect burger 28
  sweetcorn fritter burger 31
butter beans: lamb cutlets on
  mashed butter beans 88
  pork, chorizo and white bean
  stew 42
buttercream, Swiss meringue 146
buttermilk pancakes 12–13
butternut squash purée for sceptics
  166–7

C

cakes 142–3, 159
  the ambassador's cake 149
  apple and hazelnut streusel cake
  134–5
  brownies 150
  Herman's rhubarb cake 160–1
  ice-cream birthday cake 156–9
  plum and almond little cakes 151
  triple-layer lemon cake 144
  vanilla fairy cakes 147
carb-dodging mini quiches 115

cauliflower: cauliflower and quinoa
  burger 33
  cauliflower-cheese soup 38
  cauliflower purée 98
  midwinter salad 62
Châtellerault, brocante 14
cheese: artichoke and spinach dip
  169
  asparagus risotto with pea purée
  104
  baked Camembert with herbs and
  roasted spring onions 183
  buffalo mozzarella with blood
  oranges 55
  butternut squash purée 166–7
  carb-dodging mini quiches 115
  cauliflower-cheese soup 38
  cheese and pickle sandwich 111
  cheese boards 176
  cream cheese and ham sandwich
  111
  feta, herb and roasted tomato 111
  fried gnocchi with mozzarella and
  cherry tomatoes 36
  giant chicken pie 175
  Glamorgan burger 32
  grated potato gratin 48
  Greek salad 114
  halloumi and persimmon salad 64
  huevos rancheros 24
  jamón, mozzarella and basil 172
  LibertyLondonGirl's salad 52
  mini macaroni cheeses 46–7
  mushroom and halloumi burger 31
  mushroom lasagne 70
  mushrooms on toast with white
  beans 79
  puffed-up bread pudding with
  cheese and ham 43
  queso fundido 184
  Saturday-morning omelette tortilla
  wrap 23
  super-long cheese straws 171
  Superbowl avocado and bean 169
  sweetcorn, cheese and bacon
  muffins 17
  turkey gratin 74–5
  see also goat's cheese
cherry Eton mess 132
chicken: baked chicken thighs 80–1
  bang bang chicken 179
  chicken and root veg tagine 44
  chicken noodle salad 114
  chicken, orzo and parsley soup 39
  chicken salad 114

ACKNOWLEDGEMENTS

My list of people to thank was so long that it was in danger of forming a chapter in itself. Since I started LibertyLondonGirl in 2006, I have been astonished by both the kindness of friends and the support of strangers, not least from within the blogging community.

I'd like to thank my readers, without whom this book would not have been possible. It was their thousands of Tweets, comments and emails asking when I was publishing a cookbook that spurred me on to finishing the recipe book I had first started writing in 2001.

There has always been food on the blog, but it wasn't until 2009 when two men and two Basset Hounds from Colts Neck, New Jersey swooped into Manhattan in their SUV and kidnapped me for the summer (which turned into autumn) that I really started to focus on writing recipes on LLG. So to my darlings: Jason Grenfell-Gardner and Yoann Ricau, and Max and Finchley, thank you for the support, the kickass kitchen, and the picking up of the grocery bills.

There would have been no book at all without the extraordinary team at Quadrille. Extra special shiny thanks to Jane O'Shea, to my editor Céline Hughes, who has the patience of several saints, to Nicola Ellis, who designs like a dream, and to the wonderful Ed Griffiths who knows what's what.

Curtis Brown in London have held my hand all the way. Without my first agent and dear friend Richard Gibb, whose unwavering faith in me gave me faith in myself, and my literary agent, the ineffable Gordon Wise, who kicks me into touch with much charm, *FFF* would never have made the leap from my head to paper. Likewise my crack CB agent-ing team: Jacquie Drewe, Vanessa Fogarty and Fran Linke, and Team LLG: Briony Whitehouse, Katie Bowkett, Katie Rose and, most importantly, Emily Cunningham, have all helped me turn LLG into my second career.

I would like to thank Jane Bruton and Hattie Brett for helping me give up my blogging anonymity in the pages of *Grazia*, and launching me on this adventure in such inimitable style.

Jackie Dixon for making me move to New York in the first place, and for the sterling friends I made in my years in the city. Not least Rachel Carroll, Shayne Ebudo, Judy Kim, Jill Mahmarian-Fields and Carol-Anne Turner. You guys kept my head above water mentally and physically, and I will never forget it.

My life would be a barren place without my girlfriends. In particular I want to thank the ones who have helped me get this book finished, from recipe testing to gin consumption. They are Brigitte Atkinson, Meriel Bruce, Anne Fousse, Hannah Hayes-Westall, Ayla Master, Clare Shaw, Tara Spring and Philippa Wright.

Launching a blog, and then a business on your own, with no money or external investment at the beginning – and then keeping it going for eight years now – equals a lot of highs and lows. There have been some wonderful people who, although they may not have realised it, gave me the oompf to carry on. So thank you variously for support, advice, commissions, belief, and press coverage: Sam Baker, Navaz Batliwalla, Helen Brocklebank, Colin Byrne, Josie Carol, Hannah Clifford and all at Wild Card PR, Suzannah Crabbe, Michael Donovan, John Franklin, Kara Goodley and her team, Saska Graville, Seth Haberman, Jane Harper, Lizzie Harper, Laurent Kretz, India Knight, Helena Lang, Lauren Laverne, Sadie Mantovani, Diana Massey, Louisa McCarthy, Jenny McLaughlin, Virginia Norris, Caroline Perham, Lucy Perceval, Lucinda Pride, Liz Roscoe, Baukjen de Swaan Arons, Matt Rudd, Beth Schepens, Amanda Selby, Lauren Sherman, Richard Storer, and Anna Vale.

And last but not least, Peter Beckett, Elizabeth Cochrane, Joanna Richmond, Russell Taylor (who first encouraged me to write a cookbook all those years ago), Chloe Beeney, Tony Borer and Barry Dougdale, Rosalind Crossman, Rachel Eastwood, Mark Hayes-Westall, Lisa Lamb, Michele Law and Henry Knowles, Maria, Emily Moore, Sarah Miller, Emma Mosley, Rodger and Christine Newman, Rollo Ross, Laetitia Rutherford, Bumble Ward, Justine Ragany, Philip Shaw, Vicky Silverthorn, Dave Smith, Athena Skouvakis, Francesca Todd, and John Waterlow.

Thank you to Green Pan, Lavenham, Billington's, Green & Blacks, Le Creuset, Kenwood, Nespresso, and Sevket Gokce at Parkway Greens for their support during the writing of this book.